THE STUDENT START-UP

This book is written with a lot of satisfaction. While I was planning to start up there were few guides available on how to work while in college. I learned many things during the journey and have gone through a lot of mistakes. Now, I am happy that the new students are getting on how to create a start-up at college.

THE STUDENT START-UP

Become a student entrepreneur without leaving campus

AMAL RAJESH

I dedicate this book to my parents who supported me in my journey. To the teachers who created steps for me to climb up from my childhood. My friends who always wanted to be seen as happy and capture all my dreams and everyone who entered and exited my life gave me beautiful experiences and made me stronger.

How to use this book.

This book contains an action-oriented approach to start-ups. This book is most informative and many concepts and steps explained may be new to you. I request you to take off with a pen or pencil and underline the important concepts. After completing the book just flip the pages and see the values you received from this book. I assume after reading this you can start your venture and for some others who have already started up, this book will give some additional tips to be implemented. Business is a combination of many skills, mindsets, and management and so on we cannot start after getting everything but we can also learn after we have taken our first step

INDEX

"I think a simple rule of business is, if you do the things that are easier first, then you can make a lot of progress."

Mark Zuckerberg

Founder / Facebook

1

START-UP

You might have some idea about this term so you might have chosen to read this book. Start-up is a small company that might be at its initial stages of operations. Usually, start-ups have a very small team, very low funding, and maybe one or two products during their initial time. A start-up is highly different from a conventional business. For example, if you start a company where you buy products from one place and sell them in another place and gain a margin that does not come under a start-up but is a conventional business. Start-up is when the business is more innovative, bring something new products and innovation to the market, that never existed before. Start-ups also integrate several new elements to make a new product or even bring something new of all time to the market that is a lot more innovative.

The business model of start-ups is very different from a conventional business. Start-up may not be profitable from the first day in some cases whereas the conventional business's total focus is on profit. They are looking for high market share, increasing customer satisfaction, and selling their products in huge volume. Once they manage to acquire a great market share and customer base with a small profit percent, they create by selling their products will ultimately lead to a huge sum of money. That is why start-ups are getting so much appreciation. Many companies have successfully implemented them and made huge numbers in revenue.

Start-ups bring in the most innovative ideas that the world has not witnessed so far and make them to reality. Since the idea is new, not all must have knowledge or awareness about the new product, therefore the risks are also high as the rewards. At the beginning stage, they might have only a few products and the resources are limited. If this small number of products is not accepted by the audience, the company itself falls miserably. The founders will find it difficult to keep the company alive. The actual data says the failure rate is very high compared to the success part. The reason for failure is due to many reasons, they will be discussed in the following chapters.

Before you start up, you must understand what you are going to do. Not everything can be received from any book or materials but a lot of them can be found in your way ahead. The advantage of understanding is that it reduces the risk associated. You will make the maximum right decision at the right time therefore the chance of failure will be low. That is why start-ups are places where hard work pays off.

1.1 Advantages and Disadvantages

You must be clear about the advantages and disadvantages before going ahead. They may be varied from person to person. That is, the way a business expert see is different from a student's perspective it will be different for a risk taker and a non-risk taker.

The pros include

- Can become a part of creating something.
  The world has been a place for consumers which is why job opportunities are fewer and unemployment is high in most countries. The number of businesses producing products, or entrepreneurs is low compared to the population. While working in or for a start-up you can become a part of something that is going to solve a person's real-world problem by making their

life easier. Everything depends on the decision you are making now.

- More opportunities to learn
  In terms of a founder, must be a continuous learner he must be learning about the current and future trends, and the changes coming in technology. Then only the company can sustain itself, in the long run, consider the start-up as a war it depends hugely on the leader. How the leader makes the decision will be reflected in the output of the war. To make the right decisions the leading warriors must be highly updated in the domain they are working.

- Workplace benefits
  When we check the starting of the world's greatest companies like Apple, Meta (formerly Facebook), and Amazon they all started in small spaces similarly today most start-ups have very low investments, that too in infrastructure or office space at the beginning of the whole team may be working remotely. This benefits the company to reduce expenditures and make profitable earlier so the team can work at their loved destinations.

- Increased Responsibility

  Once you have started up you are no more a layman you are the founder/CEO or any chief position in your company. The whole life of the company depends on the decision you make. So, the responsibility is high once you have begun to start building your dreams.

- Innovation is encouraged

  Innovation means bringing something new or trying to make changes in existing norms and creating something new that has never been seen before. Decades before there were no start-ups there were only businesses. Start-ups were an innovation in the field of business similarly all aspects of innovations will be encouraged as the company needs new ways to create max output in low time this will not be possible in conventional business methods.

- Flexible Hours

  The work may be hard, but no one cares about how long you have been working or when have you worked. It all depends upon how smartly you worked in your time. You may be an early bird or a night owl the whole depends on what you have done during that time. So, you got great flexibility in your work. Even if you were busy with some other stuff still you can complete it late at night. There will not be a fixed 9-5 job.

The start-up is not only about fascination but also about a lot of dark sides. More than the returns you are expecting may not be received. You must be aware of the dangerous situation of start-ups. We cannot move forward avoiding them.

The cons include

- Risk of Failure

  The risk always comes with rewards. The higher the risks higher will be the reward. In the case of startups, the risk is unavoidable what we can do is to maximum reduce the risk involved. The confidence for any task comes with the experience we have in that domain. For example, while driving a car for the first time you will be highly nervous, but this won't happen in your hundredth time, that is because you have used to it. Similarly for a startup, the first time will make you fearful, and self-doubts can haunt you but once you have started or taken the initial steps with the right knowledge this will be easy for you if not in the first then thereafter.

- Raising capital and investments

  As mentioned above the starting will always be the hardest part. Once you got an idea and started to work on it the next main thing will be on the capital. You need to raise money to continue the journey since being a newbie will be a difficult part. You find it very difficult to tackle this situation. So how you can raise capital for running your business will be explained in the coming chapters.

- Stressful work

  There won't be any comfort zone here. Only hard work will pay off and there is no substitute for it. You must deal with a lot of headaches each day dealing with your team, investors, etc. So this part may be very stressful also the initial team may or may not be experienced so you have to take care of them. You have to sacrifice your sleep, and may have to work late nights and early mornings to complete the task. You might have to sacrifice the leisure time of your life with friends and family this all collectively leads to a stressful job. The way to tackle this is by being passionate about what you are doing and whatever you are doing must bring enthusiasm and excitement while going forward.

- Competitive business

  How smart or innovative your business idea will not be something that none have done or doing. The innovative idea that has not been seen by anyone is the rarest part of the game. There might be high competition in your field, you must be competitive to make your company alive. But some tactics can make you win big in the competitive market; this will be discussed in the coming sections.

"Having first mover advantage is over-rated. Myspace was the first mover. It's more important to have an idea BEST than have it FIRST. There is always room for disruption. Constantly better yourself,

To stay ahead of the game."

Jack Dorsey

Founder of Twitter and Square / Twitter

2

WHY YOU SHOULD START-UP

This must be the first question you must answer when you start up. Unless and until the purpose vision and goal or the journey are established it is difficult for you to move ahead or might face blocks in your journey. The reason to start up varies from individual to individual. This depends on the knowledge you have and the exposure you had in the past. The journey of an entrepreneur is not depending on a particular skill. Entrepreneurship is the combination of many skills. Some of them you may not possess at the beginning but the rest you will acquire in the journey. Just because someone from your circle has started up or someone has become successful and made a lot of money that does not mean, even if you do the same steps, you will be successful. They depend on your attitude, dedication, perseverance, etc. And so you must establish why you start up before you start up. So, some of the common reasons are.

2.1 To solve a problem

As we have mentioned in the first chapter start-up is to solve a real-world problem through innovative ideas and making them t reality. Not everyone can be a problem solver. Finding the right solution is a hectic task to create and implementing it in the most optimized way is even harder. But some people want to see others happy by solving their problems and that makes them happy. The people like these come under the problem-solver category. They work super hard to create a solution for a problem and finding or spotting a problem in this world is also not an easy task. As far as a nation like India is considered the business will make money only if they help Indians make money, which means they will spend only if there is an offer or so which helps them make money. Here optimization of solutions is not pay off. So even if a solution is identified to make money out of it is even harder. To make the concept even simpler this can be done with an example.

Before Uber came to India there were taxis here and people are paying for the taxi but the problem was people have to wait for a long time to get a taxi, after the coming of Uber anyone can order a taxi and the nearest one will pick you fast so Uber solved the problem of delay. And people are paying for saving time.

2.2 Passion

These are the people who won't get tired event after Woking the whole time. These people will show the difference between people who work for money and those who are passionate. You must check if you are passionate about starting up. Even if the business doesn't make money for years, will you continue because of passion? In the hard times when the hopes are wiping off things are getting out of control will you still hold on to it because you started it because you are passionate?

If you look at the world-famous entrepreneurs who are working because of passion, look at Steve jobs, Richard Brandon, Elon musk, and Mark Zuckerberg, they have got enormous wealth in their life, and do you think still they work for money? They are following their passion and building their legacy. After many years and they will leave this world they will still be remembered. Because they invested their time in building and following their passion.

2.3 To create something

Have you ever thought of the history of this world? Who is still remembered among billions of people who had lived in this world? Not all are remembered. Just look back those who are remembered till now are remembered for creating something they have established something in their lifetime and so you too can. You can work on something so hard that, that will make you remembered and make yourself proud. So in the olden ages of retirement, you can either think back to these golden days when you have created something and people are respecting you or have a regretful feeling of not doing something once you had this opportunity. This regret is faced by most people. If we talk to retired people and ask them what their life's biggest regret is won't be making money or having a good family. It is the opportunity you missed and at that time for not having strong regret you can start now.

2.4 Start-up work culture

The work culture in start-ups is entirely different from that of a corporate job. As mentioned in the first chapter this gives great flexibility and you get a chance to work with similar likeminded people who are passionate, working with such people is truly different from working with people who work for money. There you won't think of the clock ticking because you are not bothered about time passing by. You are fully involved in the work. You will see real happiness once you see the results, or you try to get a new client. This is different from working for corporates where you will be happy when you receive the paycheque every month. Start-up always promotes innovation so the skilled people who can showcase their hidden talents can come front of start-ups.

2.5 Personal growth

You don't even have to exit successfully from a start-up. You have lost a ton of money but still, achieve great personal growth. The journey itself from a normal student or person to an entrepreneur will make you a better-educated person. You will be experienced you will likely make fewer mistakes than normal. You have gone through last-moment rush dead ends and so on still in the end one way or the other this will pay you off. This cannot be achieved while you work for someone else. Your whole effort might get lost. Just think of a teaching job they are not at all updating or achieving personal growth they are still repeating the same content they are years ago not even the location is changing. Only the students are changing but, in a start-up, you must be updated day to day. Must leverage the use of the internet to tie up with the day-to-day changes in technology your competitors and so on. You will have a great professional life once you end your career in a start-up and this will be worth more than those working in other sectors.

"Pick a good market. The idea for approaching that market may change, but find a meaty problem to solve. You can try to attack it a bunch of Different ways. Don't be too narrow."

Caterina Fake

Founder / Flickr

3

STARTING-UP IN COLLEGE

This might break the norms of many businesses where the say you must gain enough experience before starting up. But that is completely wrong. People have so far proved they are wrong. In the case of students while they are in school or college this is the best time to start up, there are several reasons to strengthen this argument. If you ask every entrepreneur none will say you must start up only after you gain all experience and the ideas, or the works never came fully formed they will only be complete in your journey you have to make changes in your decisions then only great businesses can be formed so you must start at your college this might be risky and entrepreneurship is all about your ability to take the risk.

3.1 Very young age

The timeline of your life has been limited. While the time you are reading this just take a moment to think about what you have done in your life so far. And what other people your age are doing. You might surprise by what they have achieved. This is just because they have started early. If you find this book at any stage of your life, feel it as a blessing, that you can start now. There is a saying "the best time to plant a tree was 10 years ago the next best time is now". The difficulty you are going to face cannot be undone and you must face the failures at the early stage so that you can win fast. If you are starting in your 20s you will be doing more than those who started in their 30s in your 30s. You will be aware of current changes in the industry so in the later yours this will be useful to make decisions.

3.2 Time to make mistakes

As mentioned earlier mistakes are unavoidable and this is the time to make mistakes. You might be living with your parents they might be taking care of your essentials and tuition fees and so on. Now you don't have to raise yourself or pay anything just live under this shadow you can grow to a great extent and once this shadow is moved and you are liable to pay for yourself this will pay off. Even if you fail in the first place there is time for you to go next or to correct your mistakes and fail again this time make sure you have not made the same mistakes, also try to learn from the mistakes of others this is the best way to make yourself stronger. While you are hiring your first team making your first product, selling it, or in marketing even in finance part you are likely to make mistakes in the first go, my advice for you is to leverage the true power of the internet whatever problems you might face that might be faced by someone in the internet so you will fix them once you replicate the same thing in your problem.

3.3 Find like-minded people

The business cannot be done alone, in most cased you will need a team to make your idea come true in various domains. You will have to go through various ways to find such people like interviews, personally working, and finding in public, so in the end, you will find the right likeminded people in your team. You may not know everything in detail about your work. You will have to hire people who can do that for you. Once you got them there will be an exchange of ideas on all topics. May be the core team have 5 or 6 chiefs of various domain they may be expert in their respective field. In the exchange of ideas, you are most likely to get shared knowledge and information from experience which is beneficial for everyone on the team. You will know each of them in depth so you can make use of them for your future ventures also. This is the most beautiful effect of working with likeminded people.

3.4 Clubs and associations

Being in college there is more likely several clubs which is functional, and you can work with all of them. Their full advantage can be utilized. This is also a great place to find people to work in your company and find suitable brains. In each of these clubs, the faculties and alumni will join, there a lot of exposure can be created. This will be helpful in your long-term journey. You can build your interpersonal skills like leadership, team player can be all created here, you can take charge of various events and complete them successfully this brings on confidence to do something more and great things ahead.

Here also there is nothing for you to lose whatever you achieve is all benefits. In your college even if you are not preparing for a start-up this will be a great thing to improve yourself. You will gain more knowledge than what you have learned in your textbooks.

3.5 Access to knowledge from professors

The best way to learn the dos and don'ts is from the people who have done it in the past. So, professors are the best for your career development. They might have great networks from your institute or other institutes. They have achieved this in their lifetime, you can make use of them for building your network. You can ask them for guidance and when you feel self-doubts aged people are always best to fix this issue.

The professor does not mean all are equally capable you must find the right one who Is supporting you and are enthusiastic in your journey, not all teachers may be skilled with business knowledge and expertise some teachers can help you in your communication in your technical skill and all, so make use in maximum from them

3.6 Great experience

College start-ups are not everyone's game not everyone can do it. If you are doing this, pat yourself on your back because you are doing above many of them. Even if you have failed in your start-up, the experience you gained so far is enough for you to succeed in your life. When going for a job or so you are more likely to get selected because you have the work experience. Team player skills, leadership, prioritizing, public speaking, negotiations, and so on are always the greatest assets that are going to pay you in the long term.

3.7 Lot of time

On deciding to become an entrepreneur, you have to make up for the studies that are somewhat difficult for most, the excuse for most students not starting is also the same reason they have exams, attendance, marks, and a lot more but if you prioritize the college studies are those where you have to invest the very low amount of time because the knowledge you are receiving is very limited. I.e., when you opted to study science commerce may be completely out of your field. You, yourself will think that this is not your cup of tea, but this is a misconception. The people studies science, commerce or anything is the same as you. If you want to learn what you don't know, just invest more time in that subject and understand it passionately. Once you start doing it you will understand that everything in the world can be learned on your own and that what you have to invest is your time, and time becomes your most valuable asset

3.8 Cheap and inexperience labor

In college the students may be the same age group and not all can do what you are doing which is building your own company, and there may be students who strongly wish to work for experience. In case you don't find the right people, you can use them to give them a chance to work for you. The people like these will be charged less or nothing, you can find creative people and can make them in your designing and branding team, similarly the tech guy around you, this won't be made to reality once you left the college.

USE THIS SPACE TO THROW YOUR IDEAS IN YOUR MIND SO FAR

"Solve a real problem that creates real value in the world. Focus on the problem => solution => value => profit chain of events, and try to make a pass through this sequence sooner than later. Also, be strategic. Find a competitive advantage. At dribble, we stumbled into ours – we were just building a side project, but it was a site for designers, and Dan is a designer with lots of recognition and credibility. As a result, we attracted a great set of initial users who posted incredible work. Things snowballed from there."

Rich Thornett

Co-Founder / Dribble

4

BEING PASSIONATE

You might have heard this "love what you do and do what you love", this simply refers to being passionate about your work. Not only in work but anywhere in your life love the work you do. This brings happiness to your life. The happiness gives you a sense of completion. You might have heard that finding the purpose of your life, that a very few have got in their life. Try to make these words true. Passion has a lot of myths around it. If you are complaining about what you are doing that is not your passion, if you are doing it for anybody else, or if you are doing that for money then that is not your passion, passion is something that means you are doing it for yourself without looking at the clock and the paper notes you receive for it. This must be your happiness, doing anything without being tired, even if you work for straight long hours and still don't complaint and continue the task again the next morning then that is your passionate domain. "if you are passionate about what you are doing you will work till late night and wake up early to complete it".

Don't start up if you are not passionate. If you can't work all time until the task is completed or the goal is achieved, you will face many situations where things won't go according to your plan and you might feel frustrated the same, at that time you have to remind yourself that this is the part of growth, the problem you are facing now is becoming the problem only because you don't have the solution right now. You most probably will receive it in the near time then your problem will be solved to keep yourself remembering these things you must be passionate about.

Your team might not find you all passionate but if you are passionate and sincerely working towards your goal, the team will automatically find their passion and let them follow it, holding to unpassionate people will never create any great output even though how strict you are. But if you are lucky enough to find passionate people for the right job then half the work is done your job is to show them what their passion will drive them to complete the tasks and achieve your mission. The whole world has been competitive, and you have to work more than others then only you can reach the top. Do you think someone who is not interested in doing anything became the leader in anything? Think about anyone in the world from Abraham Lincoln to Elon Musk they have been passionate about what they are doing. So only go ahead with start-up and read the followings.

4.1 Passionate to self-learn

If you are someone in your college or just exited studies and thinking your education part is over in your life, sorry to say you my friend this is not your piece of cake. You must do something to find your passion by doing many things. Entrepreneurship means moving first firmly, confidently, and passionately. You cannot fight with tomorrow's world by having decades behind in education. To create something for the future you must be up to date with the changes that happened and happening in the world so you can overtake the rest and win the race. Even if you have identified a product and found a solution if you have low knowledge of the topic than your competitor, you might have won the competition and the market, sorry to say this is not to make you feel entrepreneurship is hard but to give on an insight to yourself to work on so that you can leap ahead than many others

Self-learning includes learning on no one is going to tell you to learn this or that. You must find what is needed for you and find sources for that and learning analyzing and apply. Thus, that part gets solved as simply as that. Maybe you don't know what taxing and pricing your product is, for example, you don't need to go to any organization for help first. Go to your best friend's google, and ask him if he has an answer for all your questions then comes the main part, make answers your own which means you might have seen tons of answers to your question from various people on the internet make sure you are following the right one in your situation, I have mentioned earlier you might not make it the first, second or even in the 20th go but might be in your 21st attempt if you have mastered this then there will be a solution to many of your similar problems and this is called self-improvement once you see this, you gain the confidence so that others problems are small in front of you.

4.2 Passion for Entrepreneurship

You might like working a lot of time or just working 9-5 and earning a good salary the whole choice is yours, but I have only one thing to say if you have the passion to do something you are curious about business and related stuff never settle for a 9-5 job and make the world regret losing a genius. Instead, polish the diamond inside you and shine throughout the world. If you are a person who is not willing to take risks, self-learn, or cannot handle issues, then please don't go with entrepreneurship and make you regret seeing the difficulty in your journey. Just think about yourself and find out what is think you do most of the time without being compelled by anyone then exist a passion.

As mentioned above this is a competitive world and no one care about you to make your dreams come true you must make your dream to reality by using others. You have to go through a lot of roads which may or may not be much traveled by others. In the end, you must be happy with whatever the thing you love to do.

4.3 Finding your passion

Till now in this chapter, I have talked a lot about choosing your passion but there might be questions like aiming to live my life for so many years still now I could not discover my passion this is not your problem, many people around you have not discovered theirs. So, neither you are. If everyone is working on their passion, you might have found it by the time you are reading now.

Frankly saying there is no shortcut or straight road in reaching or discovering your passion for those whom you see as passionate in doing what they are doing now is the end or output of their long findings, their starting might not be like to become an entrepreneur politician an engineer or so but at a point of time, they have discovered that this is what they love and working and building on it without being tired or lazy. Even if you are loving what you are doing now don't forget to experiment with new and stay updated with the world. If you have not yet found anything to do in your life, I have a solution for you. Look at your web history, and YouTube history and look for what you have been searching for or where you are investing you large portion of time, this topic may not be hundred percent accurate but the result of this can lead you to your passion.

Something that you may be Woking on today, may not be a passion for your lifetime. Example for people who are interested in writing articles and publishing in magazines during the olden days, can now shift to blogs for writing as people interested to read have reduced drastically on paperbacks and people are relying more on the digital screen. Imagine if the person doesn't want to change himself and said this was his passion and he won't let them go he might have overtaken by his competitors by those who have huge audience base, there are similar situations for photography also from the film camera there may be perfect photographers but the digital revolution in the camera had made a huge impact in that industry, those who were leaders during that time have to learn this technology so fast, and the situation was like they cannot do ahead without updating or have to accept defeat, failure and get out of the system, by this I have to conclude that even if you are working passionately on your jobs stay updated with the world and whichever position you may be in try to be the leader in that by constantly innovating and hardworking. There is no shortcut or easy route for passion and happiness for it. And the day you are finding it will be the day you will be thanking yourself. You will find a reason for you to live in this world.

"The joy is in getting there. The beginning years of starting your business, the camaraderie when you're in the pit together, are the best years of your life. So rather than being so focused on when you get big and powerful, if you can just get the juice out of that... don't miss it."

Barbara Corcoran

Investor / Corcoran Group

5

ENTREPRENEURSHIP

First, I would like to thank you for going ahead. Pat yourself on the back because you have taken the initiative to try something new and for taking the risk in life to achieve more. You are determined to start a start-up. If not determined and just thinking of becoming an entrepreneur be determined here. Here we are going to discuss what an entrepreneur should be like, his goals, contribution to society and to employees in creating new opportunities for the world.

Entrepreneurship is the ability and quality of a person to run a business bring on innovative ideas to reality, take risks, manage people, give employment, and so on. They provide an inevitable part in the growth of the nation as well an economic stability. They are known to bring changes in the market with the support of technology and replace conventional systems. An entrepreneur is different from a businessman. If you start a normal grocery store in any place you won't become an entrepreneur but if you bring a new system, there in the dispense of the product or anything like that then you will become an entrepreneur.

In short, an entrepreneur is a person who starts an innovative business with determination and will and is ready to accept all risks on their way will become an entrepreneur.

5.1 Skills needed for an entrepreneur

This topic cannot be explained in any sub-part, a whole book can be dedicated to this. The negative part is that if you read thousands of pages on it you can't master it until and unless you work on yourself. This section aims to give you an insight that these are some of the skills again every skill needed for an entrepreneur is a topic for another book. Here we will be mentioning the key skills and trying to master or include them in your daily life use them everywhere you are, so they become a part of your life.

5.1.1. Business management skill

Management plays a crucial role in business this can either lead to success or failure. The management alone can sometimes bring a company up or down. Management includes combining product marketing, finance, and all aspects of the business. The sale and even the service of a product. So, managing needs to be very strong. Strong business management has involved knowledge in every sector of the business. If any of the staff or a person cannot do his work the operation of the business must not get disturbed. In the first place, this might not be easily possible. You need to hire people with the skills to complete the task but make sure with time you gain knowledge in that domain too. This doesn't mean you must replace him and work there. You must at least understand what he is doing and never get cheated by anyone or you lose supremacy in your business.

5.1.2. Communication and Active listening skill

You cannot get things going and achieve your goals without proper communication. You must be a strong listening as well as a powerful communicator. Our words and actions must bring up the total energy of the team. You might get the best idea may be in your craziest time, Every time make sure is there any spark there for you to build up. Be a strong leader in your words let your intensions be strongly conveyed through your words and become a strong team player. Learn to speak according to the situation don't be that stupid leader who opens his mouth just to shout at employees. Become the role model for your firm so that the employees will wish to become a person like you.

5.1.3. Risk taker

There is no reward without any risk so for every business, if there is a risk associated with it you must be a risk taker then only you can go ahead. At any point in time, there will be a situation where you must take the risk or play safe. Keep this in mind luck only favors those who took the risk at that time. But make sure in your life you take only calculated risks. Whatever position of responsibility you are taking you must be aware of how much is your risk and how much is your reward. Take only if your rewards are more than your risk and if you can manage your risk even in the worst situation never take risks blindly this will lead to the greatest destruction of your business Empire. Society may not help you to be a risk taker they always want to be on the safe side which is the psychology of human beings. Being an entrepreneur it's your responsibility to bring your business to the top of the world. Then there will be healthy competition, so you just take it with them. You must do things on your own. You try to bring on innovation for your business to succeed

5.1.4. Networking skills

Do you think you're in you are a person who can run a business from the product ideation to the product and the post services of the product that is not possible it's very difficult? With the help of other people around us who are smarter than us. You may have expertise in a specific domain that can help us in bringing great ideas to reality this shows that network plays an important role in the business sector. If you don't have good knowledge in any of the fields your connection can help in bringing your products to Reality and fixing a lot of issues to help you in any worst situation. With networking, one has another benefit like the person may have experience or have already gone to the same situation as us now. He might have survived, for us this will be the greatest learning source for you. So, in your college try to network with as many people as possible. Talk with random strangers and get to know how humans react to things. You can learn about human psychology by just talking to them and observing them. What is their point of view and how is their thinking on a product this can be helpful and can be implemented in your business as well. If you have a very poor network, then it is difficult for you to identify the right person for your business. If you have the strongest network for your business, then you can do more than your competitor. You are most probably to have a strong team to work for you because you have already identified the potential people around you as early as possible. Today social media are a great platform to build networks to find likeminded people to work with them to collaborate and learn stuff from them

5.1.5. Critical thinking

The critical thinking skill is not received by birth, but it was acquired with continuous learning and working on it. Critical thinking involves the structuring of many components of things around you which may be in management or anything where there are separated parts. The duty is to bring up. Critical thinking is a very less skill that people process but if you somehow try to master them to bring your business model, analyze the business to create customers, to create the right product for your customers, then your critical thinking part is very much more than anyone else. This will help you in creating better products for a customer and generate more demand than your competitors for your products. In your successful journey of being an entrepreneur. You must be highly logical in what you are doing everything must be rational and must not be biased by any of your feeling or emotions. This plays an important role in critical thinking, and acquiring this skill is important.

5.1.6. Problem-solving Skill

This is not as easy as you think you might think the process is easy, but you may not even identify the problem around you. At every stage of business from the ideation path to the execution, from your product reaching the market, you have to solve a large number of problems in your day-to-day operations. Every day many areas of your business will face a lot of problems so you had to be a strong problem solver. Your teammates may not solve their problems and you must have the capability to solve the problem if you are asked to. If you don't have the skill of problem-solving, they won't come to you and will do as per their wish this is a red flag for your business. If you are not taking the supreme authority of your business, if it's not going after the vision of the company and if you are not looking after the vision and mission of your business then the success chance for your business is very low. So, for every problem you, your team face, your client face, or your investor faces everything you have to be a solver for that problem at the earliest.

Easily with fewer resources and less time you can go ahead. There won't be any time when you don't face a problem if you are not facing any problems this means you are not trying to do anything new. Try to do anything new so you may face the problem and one this is solved make sure that you won't repeat that same problem or mistake. You don't have to spend your time on solving that thing again you can also assign or delegate other people to solve serious problems and you must instruct how to solve such and such problems in the day-to-day operation in any domain of a business.

5.1.7. Customer service skill

You are running the business to put money into your company, so the customer is the one who is ready to give you that money. To solve their problem or to make their life easier than before, customer service is an important skill for you to provide to your user and customer. Provide maximum satisfaction to the customer so they won't get disappointed in using your service and they must be happy to use your products or servicesmore than your competitors. There are different ways for customer service skills. If you have sold a product, make sure you are retaining the customer. You can provide post-sale services for your product. The services you are providing is also important as the product because this brings out more and more customer. The mouth-to-mouth publicity is stronger than any advertising or any marketing tactic. If a customer tells other person that your product is good, that new customer will get confidence in using your product. This cannot be successfully deployed with any other strategy. So, make sure that you are providing the customer with the relevant services they require, and they need. Make sure you are there to solve their product problems at the earliest. Think that the sale is forever you have to maintain it, nurture it, every time you can give them an annual reminder in the email, which is used very less but create great impact for that customer, the customer will again think of your product and your company in their life. You can also approach them with your new product, any new offer, or any benefits for existing customer. If you have successfully implemented this strategy whenever they need any of the products or services related to you are providing, they will come to you. So, post Customer service is very much important. If you are in the service sector, you are providing the services to any of your clients, the services. You're giving must be very much strong and good and must solve their problems forever.

5.1.8. Time management

When you are simply sitting and wasting your time think that someone other is working right now for your same goal. Time is something that everyone has in the same quantity there is nothing more for any person from the CEO of a multinational company to the founder of a small start-up with two employees everyone has the same 24 hours. The thing is how you utilize the time effectively and to do the most productive task and delegating the simple task to others can save your time. Then your time brings on success to your company you might be living in by dividing your time to hour days but trust me the smartest people on the dividing the time into seconds and microseconds and they need to complete things in minutes. Now in terms of hours or days that much managing have done on time because it is pretty sure that the time is the most valuable thing in the world and for doing business you have to effectively utilised and manage time for the higher growth and the success of your company.

Being the highest person in the company your time management reflect in the heart of the company working, how effectively you work will determine the work culture of others, If you work without looking into the clock from the time you open your eyes to the time you close your eyes your employees will also work accordingly they will never complain about their difficulties so you become be the role model in managing time to others in your company.

5.2 Importance of Entrepreneurship

5.2.1 Creating employment.

Unemployment is one of the major crises in our world. Being a start-up founder or being an entrepreneur, you are creating employment for people you are providing money for their families and they are living happily because you decided to start a business to solve other people's problems, and thereby you are solving other people's problems along with helping your team to have a dream life they wanted. You help people to bring out their potential to bring out the passion in areas of interest and workplace don't feel boring. Innovation can help in bringing new employment opportunities for others. For every person you are giving employment one way or the other, many people depending on them, may be their parents of family. They might be rewarding with your effort so if you are giving employment with a lot of people this gives a sense of responsibility in you to never give up to never go back when you are tired to start working when you are lazy and stop procrastination in your work. Entrepreneurship is not only about solving problems and creating products and services it is also meant for helping other people and being a part in their happiness. In making a healthy humans and great society entrepreneurship plays a key role.

5.2.2 Increase standard of living

When you are employing a person for the first time, he may not have the relevant experience for your work. With time working with you in any firm for a long time can increase their income which bring on an increased standard of living. When the income of the person is increased the expense also increases that the law of Economics. He will be spending more in the market so more and more business will get more money so this is another advantage of entrepreneurship. With the expansion of your business and growth of the company more people will get employment and the concept mentioned above will be running in a cycle. If your business grows, your income will also grow this will reflect in the salary or income of your employees so they will start spending more on their essentials this will help other businesses to grow so the overall economy will grow. The people will have access to a good education good health care very good shelter and so on so the life expectancy will also increase, the standard of living of their children will also increase as they get access to clean safe food and also great education for the career.

The rightly educated students will provide something valuable to the society their standard of living will motivate other people to be like them.

5.2.3. Research and Development

When more and more products are coming to the market the research and development behind them will also increase many people will get a job in the field of research and development to create a more innovative products for their customer to identify good market and what are the future growing markets. The companies are invested heavily in the research and development field. With time the things which are not possible now can be achieved in the future with the help of research and development. New technologies coming to our hands at the early stage will help in the social development of the people and to create a better word for the upcoming celebrations. Because of the early adoption to technology the history we can see the people who have access to technology at the young age or at the earliest time have more hands-on than people who are late adopted to technology these are not problems of anyone, but these are the fact that is happening around the world.

"What is the simplest version of this app that can solve your problem? When you have the simplest version in mind, you build it, put it out in the world, and see what the response is. See what people are using it for, see what they're not, and start iterating. It's not easy, but it's doable and that's the really exciting thing."

Alexis Ohanian

Founder / Reddit, Hipmunk, and Breadpig

6

STARTUP IDEA

As of now, we have seen various topics based on start-ups, the relevant skill and expertise needed for entrepreneurship. Now we can put forward our efforts in building a Start-up. Before building anything or doing anything in the world, we must be very much confident with the destination. Without a proper destination we cannot go ahead. To find a destination there must be a proper ideation and validation process. There must be some implementation to make the journey complete, so will begin with the start-up Idea formation and the steps involved. One of the main reasons start-ups fail is because of the lack of proper Idea or their ideas might eventually fail because of non-requirement. I don't want others to make this happen in this endeavor. Also, make sure the ideas never come fully formed on the journey we will add up more ideas sometimes we have to delete it and reorganize them for the successful start-up. The point is whenever we are starting, we must make it to the perfect, then in our journey, we will find new people and come up with new ideas. Innovate something that never existed before. We have to incorporate all those and we have to make a final Start-up idea before working on any aspect of the business. The first thing we need is the idea then only we can make it into Reality. Every business which is grown to become a unicorn and turned into a multi-billion-dollar business was once an idea. There is no age for you to come up with an idea you can start at the age of 10 or even at the age of hundred there is no age limit for a great idea. There is no point in saying only experienced and aged people can come up with great ideas Facebook was started when Mark Zuckerberg was 19 years old and today that is one of the top 10 tech companies in the world. Today we will be discussing six major topics that should be considered while creating a Start-up idea. If you follow these six analyses, it is pretty sure that your ideas are strong. This chapter deals with making your ideas valid and giving confidence for you to go ahead. We have already discussed how to find out problems and solutions in the past chapters.

6.1 Make an abstract idea.

As we have mentioned earlier at this point in time you must have found any problem or you might have sorted out any product for the market. The product may be done in the past or it might be the greatest innovative product. Going ahead you must have a basic idea on what you are going to do what's your product is who you are relevant customers or audiences and then step by step we can detail to make a clear idea. Here make sure you have got the maximum details about your products and services before building the product you might have an unclear idea on how it will be useful for the person who are your potential customers, will the customer beneficial in using them, will people accept this product in their life and are you targeting for daily use or occasional use and you must categorize it to which category which segment that product must come into. Demographics is an important part while building your basic idea. If you are building for a developed nation, they are valuing the product more than the money they are going to spend. For developing for underdeveloped Nations, they value the money, for the products they are going to purchasing. This difference must be there in your mind while developing products based on demographics. The ideas must also be created in such a way that you must be pretty sure on where you are launching the first product, who will be your customers initially, how will the customers accept, also must have a small competitive advantage over others, you must be very strict with the financials of your business, what will be your initial capital needed, do you have that much money,how you are going to raise than money, will your parents support in your venture, do you get any funding from your college or university, anything like that you must be very clear before the idea is made into reality. By doing this you might have an idea of which product you are creating. Maybe it's a digital product or a hardware product, an electronic product, or a mechanical product with any basic simple idea and innovation. You must rate your knowledge and experience with your products, and evaluate that do you use this product. If someone else brings it to the market.

This must be the first question your mind must go through while developing anything. If you never use this thing, then others are not going to use it. First make yourself the list of questionnaires and answer them for making your product to reality.

6.2 Relevant Market.

Now you might have a product idea in your mind, the product's relevance, and some idea of your customers you might know the thing you want to do. Now it is time for you to check whether the market needs your product. You must study the market you are going to enter, who all are the current players and understand the market competition. Check whether there is anyone else who is enjoying a monopoly. The market and the relevance of the market you are entering is very much important. Maybe your idea or your product may be good, and it may fail in the market because you have entered the wrong market at the wrong time, this might happen to new entrepreneurs, especially in a college perspective. Therefore, the market study is important. There are instances when new businesses fail because some already established businesses take over their market. Due to this, old players and businesses will get disrupted and they will fade eventually. This concludes that the market study is important, also checking the product market fit. For normal person in layman's terms, they might be worrying more about money than the features they are receiving. You must think that will the product is fulling the product market fit concept. If you are working for laymen and building premium-priced products, then this will eventually fail. If you are working for a premium customer then the number of customers will be low, but you can charge high, but the quality must be of high quality. Even in the mid-rang, you can create a great product.

There is various method for pricing the techniques and strategies that will be discussed in the coming chapters. So that you can enter with some great strategies. You can enter in any segment, but my personal recommendation is when you are starting up always make sure you are targeting which segment you are comfortable with and have confidence in. Focusing on one segment will give you more advantages than working to get established in all price sectors at once. If you begin if you are working at the highest sector, make sure you are giving at most quality for the products and services. If you have running for the layman, make sure it is cost effective and they are affordable. They must be having some great value for the money they are spending; this must drive them to a word-of-mouth marketing approach. This is the highest rewarding among the marketing strategies in the world which made enormous companies.

6.3 Market Survey

Once you have found your market and the segment what you should do next is the market survey. If you are creating products or services for students, you must talk with other students don't just randomly rush to them to say that I am going to start a business. Just talked with them normally and try to find their problem, If they are facing the problems which you are going to address and if you think you can solve that problem with your products and services, they are definitely going to pay you and going to become your future customer. If you are building products for old people don't try to talk to students or young people go and talk to old people so this is a basic market survey. Yet there are other forms for a market survey but talking with them, to a lot of people as much as possible in a limited time will give you an insight on the relevance of your products. If there are similar products available in the market, ask others about how they feel about using them. There might be disadvantages in them, may be in the pricing, quality or any other stuff, avoid these problems in your product this will definitely be an important point to keep in mind there might be competitors in almost every industry you are going to enter. As we have mentioned in the above chapter so without a competitive business, it's very much difficult to create a business in today's world. So, make the products that have competitive advantage over other and which will fit better in your market. While doing market survey don't do mistakes this is more crucial for your targeted audience. Take feedback from the most relevant people don't waste your time and energy for others. If you are creating any products for rich people don't ask people who can't afford them. If building in an Ed-tech sector doesn't ask with your working parents. Discussing with teachers is fine.

6.4 Competitive Analysis

After you have found out your market your product segments and all you next need to find is who all are the kings in the market. Who plays key role in the market, and how much percentage of market share everyone owns? Why they are getting that much market share for their products? What advantage they are having over other competitors? You must collect all this data before going ahead because once you found out the problem in the existing products and services that there is a chance for you to correct all of them and create the best and better products for existing customers in all segments. If you have created a better product except for some people everyone else will switch to them immediately. In such cases, it is easy for us to capture the market. So competitive analysis is very much important don't treat your competitors like your enemy they are really your friend. You must find out their strengths and weaknesses the opportunities and threats. You might have a clear picture of what to do and what not to do also try to figure out their history if possible. Try to find how they become the top of the respective field also make sure you have knowledge about people who have already failed in the business there might be a lot of problems. They have faced which they could not overcome so make sure you have followed the successful, and the failed.

Sometimes the existing premium product may not have that premium quality and if you are also aiming for the premium sector people, make sure you come up with the greatest quality that not even your competitor can offer also try to add something more value than your competitors can provide. Be economical for whatever you are doing and be feasible. This must not affect the day-to-day running of your business so be innovative in your business. You can become the greatest or you can create great products in the market.

6.5 Expand your idea

Now you have found out your market where you are going to create a product not it is time for you to expand your ideas with all the data you have collected so far and the ideas you have gathered from everywhere. Try to rearrange them and categorize your products into which segment the product must be. Take the right decision at the right time. The decision you are going to take now is going to affect you and help you in the future. Try to make the best decision as of now the expansion of ideas into best product-market fit founder to best market fit concepts. Try to bring out some moats for your business. From competitive analysis and the market survey you have done, there will be a set of data in your hands. Based on this data your competitive data is completed. The failed start-ups that you already found in your research can help you to create more innovative products. You can solve all the problems they have faced in the past and you can get an idea of problems that you might face in the future. You can be prepared for this while creating your products. Make sure your team is working perfectly for creating the best product. Great products must not have any technical glitch if they are working on any technical product. The product must have a basic quality that might not get damaged in normal use. Also, the price point, must be providing value for your customer's money. According to the demographic, you have interesting things to do and so on. By expanding your basic idea now, you can create a better idea or polish existing ideas for your customers.

Ideas have become more relevant for a business and the probability of getting success in the market is getting high this is how you must find out your odds of getting successful. With your start-up, there is no single shot of winning, where you can become a successful entrepreneur and create a successful start-up there. Step by step and point by point your idea will get improve and it must be very much fit for the market only in this way you can build your products and create a successful start-up.

6.6 Sketch & Design

After all these things we had done so far, your ideas might have got a lot of shape and structure now it's time for you to sketch and decide your idea into reality this does not mean you must create the product by now. But you must try to sketch it out. Try to create the outline of the product if you know designing design the product how will look like, and will they satisfy the needs of your target audience and if not modify it as per your wish and according to product market fit. If the design is perfect, you are ready to conquer the world and make your starting successful. It is possible for every type of product and show this to your targeted audience (this doesn't mean publicly sharing to all, ask them in person). Ask them whether they like the product design. Will this help them with their issues? One first thing that can be done to do general people is to take feedback from them. The corrective feedback from them will help you in improving.

Try to create a mind map for whatever you are doing first start with the products you are going to create, then the targeted audience, and the customer base, is the product fit for the customer. If yes, try to optimize it to make it even friendlier for them. Then find out the competitive loop for among the competition in the current market. Try to solve them with your products and create a strong marketing plan so that your product will get reach to the required people. If they liked this product or they can buy it from the market. After doing this you will have a visual design of the product you can visualize everything from your thought process to reality we can create and make relevant changes in this stage. So, take this part seriously and make the first real step for your product. If you are in service sector your products is your ability to capture the customers, the mind map and decision tree will help you at your confused state at some point of time, this will also let you improve and to come out with the great product.

"Never buy swag. A sure sign of failure for a start up is when someone sends me logo-embroidered polo shirts. If your people are at shows and in public, it's okay to buy for your own employees, but if you really think people are going to wear your branded polo when they're out and about, you are mistaken and have no idea how to spend your money."

Mark Cuban

Investor / Dallas Mavericks

7

AREAS OF BUSINESS

For every business in the world, there are several sectors or verticals under them, and a lot of people are working under each category for years to make their company a success. In this chapter we will familiarise the various sectors of a business. For each business sometimes a new division will come under. Some will be stronger, and we can compromise some division at some point. As per our company's requirement we must figure out what is working and what is not. With continuous research and development with working on it we must identify them. For a tech company, the investment must be given more to technical side the technical team, similarly for every company depending on the area of the business the corresponding team must be made stronger. I will list the basic areas in this business that almost all businesses must have.

7.1 Strategy

This process must be done before working on making your dream come true. This must come in your ideation process we must forecast on how our products and business must look like. We must identify the strength, weaknesses, opportunities, and threats and must analyze where the company's strength is from and where the weakness lies in so the strategy must be created in such a way that it must overcome all these weaknesses and focus more on things that provide strength to the business. Strategy truly plays an important part. Every company is linked to a mission and vision most of the time this must be different from other companies the combined effort of all the team and the chief of the company working to make this mission and vision come true. This is where the core value lies of the entire business and all the hard work lies.

Once you have started working on a business to start building products and giving them to the end customer. We must strategize the business accordingly. We must be flexible in the things this may ultimately lead to failure sometimes. If you are starting this strategy process before building a business this will be a great strength because we have to understand the big picture of our business. We can make certain changes so that the ultimate picture will become more beautiful than before. The advantage of this strategy is that in companies there is dedicated team for this strategy. Sometimes they are called brand strategists because every company is a face of any product or services they are offering. The customers have a great picture in front of them. Therefore they will be working in order to not getting their face worse.

7.2 Marketing

This is the next thing that puts money in the company's account. For every product, there must be some marketing to be done at first, especially in the beginning phase of the product. May be innovation might be a problem solver to promote your product. It is the duty and responsibility of the company to give enough marketing for that product to get attracted by your customers. Then only you can generate sales and leads through them. If we cannot do great marketing a product will not be known to the targeted audience, Marketing is something that is more crucial in linking of the promotion and sales of a product. There are several companies that are investing heavily in marketing mostly corporates and well-established MNC.

In the case of a start-up company, it is very difficult to pump that much money at the early stage so this must not make you settle in marketing. You must create other strategies, and always keep a portion of finance in marketing. In the case of marketing always stand with the latest technologies and the latest trends in the market. Never go behind the conventional model to save some penny, because that won't work in the current market and evolving trends. According to the culture of the citizen, every marketing company or agency will be studying the customer so they will be doing things accordingly. You must go with the latest method and trends in marketing. In the marketing process, there is an advantage that if you are investing some money in marketing than in human resources. Which thing can bring on more money? It is the marketing strategy for sure, at least for the modern world. The money you are investing in humans and with the adoption of technologies instead of humans this cost can be reduced to a great extent. Even in small companies, the expense may be low. So, they rely more on technology. Usually, small companies never go with a marketing strategy. If you want nice customers, try to get maximum output from your marketing.

7.3 Finance

Finance deals with the cash flow of a company as the experts say cash flow is called the king of the company. The functioning of the company in the long run, how the company will perform, whether will it sustain itself in the long run, will it have any added advantage over its competitor everything is based on how the company handles its finance and how the company is putting on investments. Where the company is putting money and from where the company is getting the money is important. If the company's income and expenses are not in sync the company might face loss and if the company might face loss it will be difficult to survive.

In some black swan events how, the company is going to survive, and the struggle is difficult. When the company is in profit the company must make other sources of income, many companies put the money and invest in some other instruments or so. We must have a great balance sheet, cash flow statement, and P&L statement for the company.

Before we have to start a project the numbers as per the reality of the present market conditions and the quality of the product must all be defined and set as the target. Now the company must work to achieve these financial numbers. Financial goals are always created by the company so that they can be broken down to the employees in their lead generation team. If a company can't handle its finances very well then, it's pretty sure that the company cannot sustain itself in the long run. If the founders are taking out more money from the company, they all are causing a threat to the survival of the company. If a company's product is not performing very much and some other product may outperform. The company can focus more on which product is providing more cash flow. Something which is going to tell in the future is that some strategic involvement, can bring the company to a great success with financial concepts ultimately every business plan for money and make profits and this is possible to achieve.

7.4 human resources

For a start-up company, the initial investment will be very high. The company might have to invest a lot of time and energy for its growth. Human resources are important to achieve the mission and vision of the company. The people who are working for that must be selected in such a way that they can make the vision and mission true. If the team cannot make something like this in the long run the company is going to face severe issues. They might have to face a lot of struggles in hiring and firing. If a team is working for a longer period, the individuals in the team must achieve excellence in the company and must have understood the culture of the company. The one thing with investing a little time and effort in human resources is in selecting the right candidate, selecting the right candidate is also important when a candidate to be terminated.

If the candidate is not performing up to the mark for a given period, he must be terminated for the growth of the company. Also, according to the efficiency of a candidate, some special candidates like a ten percentage of the employees in the whole team might be contributed to the 70 or 80 percentage of the total company's growth. In such a scenario more priority must be given to them than others and create a checklist on the evaluation of each individual. In that checklist, it must be clearly mentioned when they must be promoted or terminated. Always the team must be aware that the ultimate success of the company and personal growth relies on the combined team effort.

7.5 Technical

For a lot of companies who are working in the tech or the non-tech field that might be some aspects. In business that cannot be avoided in this twenty-first century. Most people stay on the internet today so we must show our presence there. Then only we can generate leads and create a brand for our product and company. Every company investing now in the technical team including their websites or mobile application must always show its presence on the internet at any cost because every person who is searching for a product or service must be looking for it on the internet. So, if we don't have any internet presence till now then we will be still undiscoverable in the real world. We can outsource the technical work, several other companies are providing technical services to companies this is a great plan. If you are completely a non-tech company. If you are a tech company, then 80 percent of the focus must be given to the technical concept. The technical team must be considered in creating the products. They need to be working on fixing the bugs and glitches so the working will be smooth for the customer. Technical companies soon might change the growth of the world and so a lot of people are coming to build tech products. The disadvantage is that the technology does not enjoy moat in the market (in most cases). If anyone can describe the technology and can provide a more optimized and cost-effective product, then your customers and clients will adapt to new companies quickly. It is easier for tech companies to take the companies to next level which has advantages as well as disadvantages. The overall growth has already been found that without technology a company is not able to sustain itself in the long future. Therefore every company much invest in technology.

7.6 Operation

After the company found out all these things that we have discussed so far, we must operate all these things in proper sync. The CEO is the person who takes all the execution of a business. His ideas must be done by other divisions of the company. It is the duty of the operation. The operation team will look after whether everything is working perfectly. If any of the divisions is finding any problems this can affect the harmony of the company. All the provisions must work in proper sync such that the company can provide greater services to the customers.

Operation teamwork is the backbone of every business. The operations team must be active from the first day of starting the business from the first employee entering the office to the last employee leaving the office everything must work properly and the channel must not find any traffic in between. For a Start-up Company, there won't be much investment in the operation field, but it is very much necessary, at least when the team is more as someone can look after it wholeheartedly. If there is any issue finding in any of the workings of an employee or the operation of the company, they can be compensated with a great panel of experts who can find external help. Everything must be done by this operation team and must ensure that the team is working properly so that the output of the companies is at its maximum.

"What I learned from Rockefeller that's off-the-hook important is: You need to know exactly where you stand in a business at all times. Measure everything, because everything that is measured and watched improves."

Bob Parsons

Founder / Go Daddy

8

BUSINESS PLAN

We cannot get started without knowing the destination this is similar to the case of business, every business has some plan but the problem is, it won't be structured well-curated, and professional. So, it is very important to create a business plan this not only helps you in your journey but also all areas of business. This will help you to be thorough with you your journey. There won't be confusion going ahead and this helps in the smooth journey and avoiding obstacles in the journey. The plan must be created in such a way that, what all things to be done at what time, sometimes at the beginning stage there won't be much focus needed for something so that effort can be transferred to the things which need high importance.

8.0 Types of Business Plans

The business plan can be classified into two based on the appearance and the creation of the Businessman. The first one is the conventional business plan created for the traditional business. In a traditional business plan, there will be a lot of pages ranging from tens to even hundreds of pages but in modern times they have become invalid as most people prefer time over other things. There won't be any time available for everyone to go through each page and every paragraph so this is the conventional and traditional business plan, The advantage of this conventional plan is that everything will be explained in detail, after going through the entire business plan the person will get the complete idea of the business and their products and services. They give more direction to business owners in business operations.

The other business plan is called the single-page business plan where all the aspects of business plans are clubbed and they have incorporated into a single or a few pages. This can save a lot of time and can be more appealing to the investors only the important points are mentioned in this business plan the invalid points are removed and making the business meeting crisp and clear. No time is wasted between the investors and the owner meetings. Single page business plan will help to reach the top among hundreds of other business plans. The strength, weaknesses, and other opportunities can be spotted easily. Their advantages can be highlighted and specified accurately. Most people prefer a single-page business plan over a conventional business plan.

Some people create both business plans because for anyone to appeal they present with the single page business plan and for in-depth information on operations and running of a business most people preferred is the traditional ones, The traditional plan might be boring and for the investors, a lot of jargons can be stuffed also a lot of valuable information can be hidden at the same. With the help of a single-page business plan, the valid points are only present, and that questions and a meeting can be made Crisp short, and clear that's what most smart people prefer.

8.1 Executive Summary

This part is the most important part of any business plan and a business plan is a strength and the route map of the entire business. Executive summary plays a significant role in the overall system plan. The executive summary comprises all the activities in the businesses in the short. This is the most important part of any business plan. Executive summary plays a significant role in the overall system plan. The executive summary comprises all the activity in the businesses shortly when you are presenting the business plan to any investor the executive summary will create an impression to go further deep in the business plan. This summarises the problem you are facing and how you are going to solve the problem by pinpointing the customer and how you are going to sell your products.

A brief description of the products and services that you provide. You can focus on the financials in a very short executive summary. You can also give a smart introduction about the market you are going to enter. Current competitors and a short note on them can all be summarised in the executive summary. The executive summary gives an impression to readers. Based on how beautiful your executive summary look, will give a picture of the strength and weaknesses of your company. How your company is performing and what your vision for the company is cannot be summarised in this executive summary.

8.2 Description of the business

Once you have given the introduction in the executive summary now it's time for you to describe the business. Describe what the business is going to do, how you came up with this idea what the problem you are solving, and what services are offering to the customer everything must be described in this section. If you are working on some tangible product. From where you are getting all the inventory, what are your investments, and which part is taking more money? Based on this, you can describe where you are investing everything can be described in this section. You can also mention the reason why your business is ahead of other competitors. What competitive advantage and in which area your strength lies?

Mention the key advantages over other products in the market and how your business is structured. How many employees will be there everything can be described in this part? By seeing a description of the business, the investor can see the real picture of what your business exactly is. From his experience, he can compare it with others. If you can prove that your business will work, the probability of you getting investment while pitching to the investor is very high also during the running of the business. If you find any difficulty in any of the structures and you can come to this business plan and see the description of your business. If your business needs improvement or changes in anything you can change it in the description of the business, but this does not mean you can shift the business from one domain to another.

8.3 The market business will operate

This part of the business plan will show the growth potential of a business. For every business, there is an upside and a downside. Every industry will boom at a particular time, and it will diminish at another point in time. It's better important for you to enter the market at the right time. Some industries will stay consistent and are always used by the customers and have demands, like FMCG, pharma, and consumable goods. Such businesses will stay on their forever I mean for a lot many years, there is no need for such obligations for such industries, but the thing is that only the established businesses will always stay and hold the market share in such industries.

For an innovator with a new idea start-up, it's very difficult to get market share at the beginning but there will be some space left in the market. During the early 90, most companies were computer companies and there was huge investment flowing to the computer company, but they did not stand for a long time and burst, and it was called the dotcom bubble. For someone who is entering the business making sure the market you are going to operate in is very important. If you are trying to bring some innovative new business model and create a solution for many audiences, the probability of you getting more appreciation is high. If you are into the conventional business model doing the set of same things, then you may not be much rewarded. The potential risk is also high.

So always try to get into the best and booming market. In the market cycle, some industries might fail at a time. Never enter the business by seeing the historical record of companies that have gained maximum profit, that was because they have already gained maximum market share and have provided the maximum services to the customers now, they are on their way to creating innovative new products for the customer. Once we have entered the market that might change. The industry might fall and ultimately the business might also fail along with it.

8.5 SWOT Analysis

SWOT stands for strength, weakness, opportunity, and threats these are all the elements of a business. A business's strength stands on what is the core values of your business. What makes your company stands out from other businesses, this can be based on the model of your business, the innovative products you are creating, it might be your team, it might be the founders of the company, and anything which is providing strength over other companies. This is also an option to show others why they should invest in your company. If your strength is something more competitive than others, then your strength can create a great impression among shareholders. For a company that occupies a shop or office, its location might be the strength of that company. Similarly, anything can become the strength of your company, this doesn't mean that if a company's number is more like in the case of employees, which will not provide the strength of the company but can also turn into a liability for the company. You can show the assets of a company the expenditure of your company and how your expenditure is compared with profitability compared with others. All this can be considered under the strength.

Weakness is also there in other parties. It must be found in the business plan. If you could not find any person for doing a particular job this can become a weakness. If you don't have any competitive advantage or anyone other than you getting to the market and capturing the market this can become the weakness of your company also this is very much important to specify. If you are specifying the weakness in the business plan. It's very good because when the investor is asking you what all your weakness is then there will be asking questions based on this. Identifying the cause of weakness is also as important as finding out the strength. Once you have understood all the weaknesses it will be easy for you to resolve the issues.

Then comes the opportunity if you have found out the best innovative solution for any problem. You must identify where the opportunity of a business lies. What is the opportunity you are capturing how you can solve the problem, if you have solved the problem how will your customers Pay you, and will the customers be satisfied with your products, if they are satisfied what we will do next and if they are not satisfied, what will you do next. You can mention all such opportunities in your business plan.

Then comes the important part of your business, because once you start there might be a lot of problems. You might be seeing a lot of them once you are creating a business plan if you can identify the maximum difficulties you are going to face, in the future, this will be very much beneficial. The other person reading the business plan must understand what all difficulties are you going to face. The advancement in technology can create a huge benefit in your current technical company. If you miss any important person in your company that can also become a threat.

SWOT analysis gives the overall picture of what are the strengths, weaknesses, opportunities, and threats faced and can be faced by the company. If you have identified all these things, you can solve the issue. Also, be prepared to face them in the future.

8.6 Management team and personal

This section of the business plan shows the management strength of the team and the company. The person behind working in creating the mission and vision, solving the problem of the people, and running the business, the personal information about the founder and chairman along with their background will give more confidence to others while reading the business plan. If the leadership team has any previous track record in working or creating something that is always an added advantage. If the team is providing great strength and the people working with them have any previous track record this is always an added advantage. The management and Co-founders and their experience give more confidence in running the business even if you have identified the great people in the market and the great opportunity. The solving real-world problem shows that person's ability to run the business. Management is also important in solving the problem which is why business is called the combination of many things.

8.7 The products and services offered

By this time, we have given the description of the business the market and everything regarding the business now it's time to show what products and services we are going to offer. In this part, you can create a forecast about the future products and services, after the growth of the company is achieved. The product can be anything mentioned in the business plan which are you are creating. The scope of our product in the future with our products can be written in the business plan. The cost of manufacturing the products can also be mentioned, and the production course of the product and at what price you are going to sell it in the market can all be described in this section of the business plan. Also, if there is any paid servicing included in your business for the further service of the product must all be mentioned here. You can also create a pie chart showing the types of production services we are creating and the expected number of customers and the revenue they are generating in each part.

8.8 Marketing

This is the important part we have already discussed a small portion in the above sections. In this section, you must create a very good plan after the products and services are created, and how you are going to reach the target audience. Now we must create a strategy for how to reach our potential customers with our products after the product reach the customer how you are going to retain the existing customers and sell the next product to them, what will be your customer acquisition cost, how you are going to acquire your customer and how you are going to treat them. The company's culture is involved better employees for their wholehearted dedication to achieving the goals.

As mentioned above what all are your marketing plan, that you are going to use this can be traditional or modern digital marketing methods as per your company audience. Using the most appropriate marketing strategy you can also outsource your marketing to other companies this can provide more efficiency to you than creating a separate team in the early stage of a Start-up. You can use highly innovative ideas for marketing, like the branding of your company to the tagline or even the carrier bags you are delivering to the customer at the time of purchase can all be added to the marketing section. Whatever you are doing in marketing can increase the sales of your company and can generate more revenue for your company. This must be done positively in your business journey so that if there is anything new and innovative strategy applied, even if the products and services are average with the help of a good marketing plan you can win the race. You can reach the unexplored part of that industry. You can also teach the customer about your products and then make them buy from you. All this can be achieved with a great marketing plan.

8.9 Financial Plan

We have done all these to create a business that is generating profit for your company. There are differences in the businesses they are operating we have already mentioned, some businesses may not be profitable in the early stage and they will be focused on creating more customer base so that they can offer discounts for the products and can capture a huge market. So, depending on the individual start-up ecosystem the business plan changes and so the financials may also vary accordingly. Y You might be profitable by different methods may be your product producing a huge margin or may be your service or both will be contributing to the profit. Some products will be making a hundred percent or even more than that percentage of profit for each product at different markets. All but there will be companies that will be making less. This is completely depending on the future of the business and the industry you are operating the income can increase as well as decrease. While creating a financial plan you must mention your capital, your capital expenditure, and your expected returns from the products, and for each product and services how much percentage of the income is generated must be created very properly. With the help of this before you create your products and services, you get a big picture of your financials, and you can work on it to create and make this forecast true and increase the chart.

With these topics combined, we can create a great business plan. As mentioned earlier business plan is the road map of your business you can always look back to the business plan make changes delete something to add something as the company grows and the team increases so the business plan must be there before starting any business

"The key aspect for entrepreneurs today is either to identify extraordinary opportunities or go very fast and build as many possible barriers of entry as they can imagine."

Ben Silbermann

Founder / Pinterest

9

TEAM

We have already mentioned the aspects of business and a lot more in the above sections in this chapter I thought of giving more focus on the great part of every start-up which is the team. For every start-up, the team will be working like a family. There won't be any 9 to 5 working there, the team must work till the goal of the company is achieved. The overall responsibility of the company is provided to everyone in the team, everyone is working as a pillar for the start-up, so they will provide the maximum in making the company to the fullest. Even if a significant person loses his skill and is not able to contribute to the growth of the company this will affect the overall performance of the company, the overall functioning of the team is very much important as well as keeping them motivated so that they can work in full swing. In College, it is very difficult to hire extremely talented people and working professionals. There are several other methods you can start up in college and can find the right team on your campus and the nearest friends to find minder people like you this will be discussed in detail in the coming sections.

9.1 Identify position

What all might be the plan, now it is time to start working on your start-up, and before working together to produce the products and services we find what to be done by whom and other elements in our starter team, a small technical, social, marketing, finance, operational team. We will identify the position for each to work in. Each sector is created for doing something. The team must strongly focus on the allotted work. We had to identify the right position and we have to maximize the resource utilization and the People's utilization then only we can produce a strongly motivated working team in achieving the mission and vision of the company and making the company profitable. Identifying the position want to have to satisfy the requirement of the company. The person has to be skilled and must be able to process and complete all the tasks given to him.

Identifying the position and selecting the people for that position is very much important. We don't need to give importance to every part of the business at the early stage. A well-created plan on how we are going to do the business and do them accordingly. Locate where the huge investment needed may be in the form of money or human capital. In this section, we must make the highly skilled and leveraged person, at that there might be chances that one person has to do multiple positions. So that's why I say that in a start-up ecosystem there is a heavy task and low pay at the beginning stage. The ones who are talking work in a Start-up must all understand this situation. There might be only one or two people working in a specific domain and someone has to look after another job also if in case of any issues absent for a small period or so.

9.2 Appointing the right work to the right guy

Once we have identified the position and it is now time to appoint the right work to the right guy because if we are not giving the right work to the desired the productivity of the person is lost forever. If the person is passionate about the creative field he must not be given work in the marketing or social domain. We must identify the potential of every individual in that company and must give and use the potential of each individual and maximize the output from them. Then only we can create a maximum gain for the company. The trading company also appointing the right to work is as important as defining the position and giving them work, if someone is willing to work more than what he was asked, appoint him to a higher position of leadership. If you have not found the right person there is no need to hire someone for the namesake in that position. This is the wrong thing that you should not do while starting. That is anyone who doesn't have the right skillset holds a position the position that he holds, and the area of the business will become the weak point of your business. We must find the most absolute and precise person with motivation for chief positions and the required skills to work in that position. If not, there is no point in acquiring and will become a liability lot for the company so it will be difficult for the other team to work with them in full swing. We need to consider the overall culture of the company while appointing. If a person is skilled and may not fit for teamwork it can affect the productivity of other people also. When selecting the person to work make sure he is highly fit for the culture of the company and highly skilled and also is the right person working at the right place.

9.3 Try to find people looking for experience

In a college in the case of an Indian campus, there will be students working for their profession and future along with their academics. They will be learning stuff outside of classrooms to build their career. They might be working in several domains on their own and now it's your responsibility to find out people who are dedicated and working for themselves and if you can find them, you can offer them a job offer that can help them to make their work a professional level and you can convince them by explaining the exposure they are getting with a lot of experience in working with your start-up and become a part in creating a great business system. This will help in their resume and Portfolio, like working in a Start-up during college is always an appreciable work during their placement. You can give awareness to them of the advantage they are getting in working with a company which only a few will receive so that they can work without looking for money and without looking at the task at any time. If you can find such excellent people working for experience and leveraging their skills for business can help you build your mission and vision. It is a great advantage that you can find in your college with the help of all these people. They will do things that they are liking so they won't be getting bored doing these things. It will be beneficial for their future and career also.

9.4 Hire slow-fire fast

Once we are hiring it must be a slow procedure we have to look after every individual to the fullest, what their time weakness, and what can they contribute to the productivity of their company this is absolutely important in hiring and once you're getting lost in this procedure you must be able to fire them as soon as possible. Carrying such people just because you have hired at a time does not mean they can provide products to the company, this can sometimes lead to reducing other people's enthusiasm and motivation to work with your company. The overall swing at the company can get into doubt. So, the total concept of hiring slow-fire fast is considered in the case of start-ups, especially in college. We might go wrong at the earliest because we lack years of experience that another MNC has. You want to hire them because of their skill culture and their value proposition even after knowing they cannot contribute significantly to the company in that case also, we need to fire them as soon as possible. There is no point in looking down the hiring process it is as important as firing for the overall growth and success of the company.

If a person is not willing to work then wholeheartedly ask to leave the company first you must listen to the reason and if you can solve them then they can continue, if they are quitting for some other reason let them do it, never hang on to someone who is not interested. For a start-up the company needs an energetic, interesting, motivational team, this is the basics. Create a great company then only ideas come into and can work with a lot of challenges that you are going to face in the journey of business and provide experience to your life.

9.5 Post-hiring

Once you have found a person for a position that does not mean that your work is over. Then your greatest work starts here you must continuously monitor that person whether the person is fit for that work or not you can give them a probationary period for their work. If your company has that potential or else if you have found out that person is not up to the mark you can immediately fire him at any cost. You must evaluate among the team who is performing best and who is performing the least and if you can find a person who is an alternative to the worst performer in your team free feel to ask him to join on board and ask the weak person to leave the company as soon as possible. The business aims to create products and services. For that, we need to solve the real-world problem of any person in the team. If the team is not flexible enough to create that mission and vision, and someone is slowing down the process he is not fit for that company. Firing is also as important as the hiring team, started the hiring procedure may be very much complicated as well, at first hiring may be done by the leadership team. Once the company has shown traction and if the company has the potential, you can outsource the hiring process there, they will have the right candidate for you. In a college if you are just starting or started then it is much easier to find the next candidate because there are a lot of students in your college itself and there might be people who are not willing to work, you can give awareness and ask them to join onboard instead of the person who is not working if a person is working to the fullest and is providing a lot of advantages of the company that gave his some appreciation token of appreciation and something so that he can stay motivated and work more, before such things and giving training to them from your limitations this is also very important as hiring

So, in the end, business is not a single-person journey it is a journey of many people working together to accomplish one common mission and vision. The team plays a significant role in building your start-up in your college days. Remember that it is easy for you to find many numbers of candidates for work but find who can work for experience and that can be beneficial for their career. Always appreciate the maximum output giving the candidate. Don't hesitate to fire the wrong ones. One day we can make a great culture for our company. If the company has a great culture then people will work without any other issues and with full power and motivation.

"Don't measure too many things. People often become overwhelmed with a deluge of data because they're looking at 1,500 variables. And that can be paralyzing because you end up sitting there looking at your analytics program all day long as opposed to doing the more uncomfortable thing that you should be doing, like calling that big customer. And usually, the most uncomfortable thing to do is the one that people need to act on soonest."

Tim Ferris

Author/Entrepreneur / 4-Hour Workweek

10

THE HARDEST WORKER

So, the work will increase once you start your company, and you must meet the deadlines. You and your team must work a full day to give satisfaction with your products and services to the clients and customers. In this section, I want to tell you something about how to work in the top position. Firstly, become the leader instead of a boss which means the leader is someone who works tremendously in achieving the goal of the company with the personal development of the team members, here the words of all people are taken into consideration and proper spaces are given to all. Proper training and the work-life balance must be provided to all. Whereas the boss is the person who will be stubborn with his work and treat others like employees not promoting their individualism and skill set.

10.1 You must know everything about the company

Since the idea of starting a business may be yours and when the team gets big and with the growth of the company there will be more people coming into your business to work and as customers, they may be assigned to different duties, since they all are different individuals, they have their individualism in business, work, and their personal life. They might integrate their knowledge, management skill, and personal experience into the business. You might need to think about diversification of business sometimes. You are working to build a strong business and you are hiring smart intelligent ones so they might have a lot of ideas than you. Once you have given them the mission and vision, they might contribute significantly so you accept the idea and include them. Since you have the power to take decisions you may not be aware of everything because you might be busy with some important tasks but anyhow you must he aware of everything that's happening inside your company might be the structure of the employees and every aspect of the business also. You must be aware of that industry and what changes and updates are happening there. After this, there might not be any work that you don't know. If you have anything and you are hiring to do that work, you must be earnt by the least time from them. In case a person is left out of your company there won't be any loss or will be stuck forming in your company. If there is some gap forming, then that demand and supply will work here this was because there will be a demand for that work, and the person who is meeting that demand that will create more strength in your company. This minor strength will lead him to supremacy in the company. The entire control and strength of the business must be in your hand, and everything must be done with your permission only. There won't be happening anything without your knowledge at the beginning time.

10.2 Absence of one person must not affect the company

There are instances in companies and happening many industries, where if one person is absent on a day there won't be anyone to replace his work. While starting up is a great challenge for the founder of the company, and this is unavoidable, and it happens. If there is no one to replace a work the pressure on one person will increase and the emotional balance of that person will also get affected and he feels the work be hectic. In some cases, he may not be able to continue with the company. Maybe he catches an offer from another company and goes out immediately the overall working of the company will be in trouble to overcome this situation you must always train other employees in such a way that they might be able to handle any situation according to the need and then there must be at least two or three people might have the potential to work instead of a single person at any job role. You must also find a substitute who is trustworthy and equally capable as yourself in your company. So that once you have been a little busy running the company or have any personal health issues for the person. You can look at the company for a long period with his help of him. With time you can also substitute him for your work this will help the company to run on its own on autopilot and your clients will not be affected. If this is not possible your clients and your customer will get transferred to other businesses. Make trust with your clients and customer responsibility your number one priority. So, you must be there at any time to solve the company's issues and further push the company to a great level.

10.3 Advantages of networking

You are the heart of the company and you have to make the maximum network for your company to grow, then only more people can be employed and turn into a more money-making business. The total networking part of the company is completely reliant upon you, there cannot be any dedicated team for that. There must be negotiated with your customers and with your networking skills you can make them in your favor. It's not the duty or responsibility of anyone else in your company so take responsibility for networking. There might be chances where you can network with people seem to find opportunities to find where your potential customers and who can help you by benefits of your business you have to find them and go to them in their available time, which may be happening in a party outside so you might find time to go and attend the party. It's not time for you to enjoy the party but to take time for that person and issue a relationship in between while building relations never go to ask for your needs. Always create a Win-Win situation for both, make a few nice and friendly conversations with that person so that they can trust you in the first words themselves.

10.4 Ownership should be taken

Once the company has grown up there might be chances you might face good times and win many awards, recognitions, and achievements and you must not only take responsibility to take awards but also take up ownership of the failures of anything happening in your business. Anything that can happen wrong maybe your product failing, cannot meet deadlines in your company take ownership of them and try to motivate the employees. Make them understand that, this is the journey and things like that happen, and advise them to learn from their mistakes and not same mistake again. This is a great opportunity to become a leader and show your leadership and empathy towards others in your business. This brings on a great culture to your company so that the other employees can copy them in their life this can bring on great employees and great employees produce a great product for a market. If the culture is very bad and the people are not loving and caring for each other they are only running behind their industry which will affect the overall output of your company.

10.5 Creative and innovative head

Since you are the founder of the company, from a creative and innovative perspective you must be ahead of others in your company. With your innovative skills during initial and tough days, you must use the least resources and find the maximum optimize way in getting things done, which you might find in the most talented people I've mentioned early to create supremacy over your company at everything, that might be people or any other resources, you want to make sure that the people together with you as productive as well. This is what we mean here by creative, for the term innovation area means that you must be innovative in whatever you are doing not just blindly follow the conventional system of other businesses on your competent you must be in the way it in your way so that the other competitors one day will follow your company's model. Then you don't want to investigate others and we can look away and go ahead.

10.6 Prioritise the needs

Once you have started working on a company that will be several needs to be satisfied some are needed by the company's team, and some for the growth of the company so you must prioritize which to be done first, and order to complete tasks. You can also make a substitution at this point you can substitute something with another so that the work goes properly. Priority is an important skill that you must adopt in your company. You have to do all these things. You not only prioritize the work but also the time for every individual the equal thing available is the time, the same 24-hour is available for Elon me and you, it's how we use it that matters for business resource utilization is also important because if we use all the resources at a time, we need to conserve them for the future. If not in case of necessity, we will be in trouble and cannot make up with the requirements.

10.7 Initial stages are more like a Jigsaw

Once you have started your company the initial stages might be a bit difficult at least for a few weeks. If you have proper planning and get a clear picture of what to do next and what to do in the latter part of the business there might be fewer challenges to face, that too with which part to be done first and not to be done now and how to hire, and how not to hire. There might be a lack of knowledge in this part of the business. Never give up and never settle with this thing. It is a part of the journey so the initial stages must be tackled if you don't know the last stage of your business, you must at least know which step to take in next so you can do the next step and if I have only one thing to say never stop and only give up until you have done it and not when you have faced some blocks. You might be also finding it difficult to prioritize assigned duties and jobs to your teammate, so these all are natural while starting especially in college, and try to overcome all these initial Jigsaw puzzles and sort at the earliest and initial stages. The structuring of the company must be done properly then only the work done will be smooth so that you don't have to work on it, to create again in the future there is only some modification to be done when you have continuously monitored the business.

10.8 Financial targets

Since businesses are associated with the profits, they are making. There might be financial targets for a team in most businesses that develop. The product needs to be marketed through the proper channel and the financials must be done properly. You can assign duties to you are subordinate and can pick the right person who makes that financial targets and if someone is making continuously their targets and got it. Give them a small token of appreciation and keep their work emotional, making them understand the role he is playing in the success journey of the company. This can also help others to meet their financial targets. If everyone is highly performing your company's growth will be phenomenal. By this method, your company's financial targets can be met on a weekly, monthly, quarterly, and yearly basis. Your company can become profitable and attract a lot of investors for expansion.

"As tempting as it may be to staff your new business with friends and relatives, this is likely to be a serious mistake. If they don't work out, asking them to leave will be very tough...One of your goals should be to find a manager who truly shares your vision, and to whom you can someday confidently hand the reins so that you can carry out the next step."

Richard Branson

Founder / Virgin

11

Legal Basics

You are going to become a start-up founder. While starting a business it is important to know the legal aspects of the corresponding companies. There will be a need for you to take certain actions and for that, you need certain contracts to be signed, certain agreements for your business account, and legal taxation. There are also several types of licensing required for business according to industry. According to industries, it is different. Therefore, you need to know the basics of the legality of your country. From a Book alone it is very difficult to understand a hundred percent. While running a business you need to find an expert in your legal processes. If the company becomes big many multinational companies have an in-house legal advisor for their business. It is as important as anything else in the long run. Running a business selling products to your customer many peoples are involved. The government must protect the rights of everyone. So, we must pay taxes according to your business tax bracket. And protect the safety security and privacy of our customers

In case you have not followed properly the rules and structure of the government it is very difficult, the people can also sew you in jail. So always follow the legal team as per the company country you to do

11.1 Business types

First, you must understand your business type. According to the country, there are several business types, you must choose which business type are you while registering your company. Some of the business registration types are sole proprietorship, partnership, limited liability company, and private limited company. All businesses must be registered under any of these types of businesses. Maybe you might get know what I am going to say, there is no business registration as a start-up it is a position of a business, or if a company undergoes certain criteria they are called a start-up(in the case of India). Start-up is something that is a company that has certain features that makes a private limited company a Start-up if you're starting a conventional business model and registering under a private limited company it's not a Start-up. For that there had to be certain criteria fulfilled by a private limited company then only the company can come under a Start-up. If you cannot register into a private limited company or a limited liability partnership at the start and register under a proprietorship firm or partnership and you are bringing the values and culture of a Start-up to your business. There is nothing wrong in doing so, it is only as per the Government of India that how a start-up must be formed so. If you cannot register like this there is no problem in creating something like this you can still create an innovative and great business and once your business has expanded you can create it on a larger scale.

11.1.1 Proprietorship

This is something I call a single-person company. The registration of this type of business is not mandatory you can register also, and no formal registration is required. Proprietorship is not recognized as a separate entity but is considered a personal work of an individual. The liability of the company will be imposed on that person and that person is liable for all good and if any bad is happening for that business. The taxation of companies comes under personal income tax (if you are falling into the tax bracket you have to pay taxes accordingly). There will be a threshold amount of turnover for a business to become a proprietorship depending on the country. If the turnover exceeds it cannot comes under this business type.

11.1.2 Partnership

This might be familiar to you the word itself is saying what the company is. A partnership is a company with legal documentation between two people running a company. The partnership is also not recognized as a separate entity both the promoters are equally responsible for all liabilities and assets for a partnership that might be a minimum of 2 people and the registration must be done under a partnership firm. It was perfectly shaped in such a way that even if more than a single person can start a business under certain conditions, so the partners can contribute equally to the growth of the company. Taxation is done under the Personal Income Tax Act of that country. Sometimes a small charge to pay to register and apply for a partnership business

11.1.3 Limited liability partnership

A limited liability partnership is also called LLP. Is another type of business registration. They are a separate legal entity where the promoters are not solely responsible for everything in the company. The company itself is an entity, the company can be accountable for its assets and liabilities. The company requires two or more people to start a limited liability company. There are several advantages to a limited liability partnership.

The risks of the founders are limited. Shares can be created. Can avail of loans in the name of the company. But there are also several disadvantages. The disadvantages there are some difficulties in starting up. The company ownership can be transferred to some other person in the form of shares for a limited liability partnership.

The returns had to be filed to the government also as per the government rules. Others can invest in your company. Even people outside the country can also invest. So, you can make foreign investments, if you have registered under a limited liability partnership.

11.1.4 Private limited company

A private limited company is also called a corporate company where to start there is a minimum of two people required. It is also considered a separate legal entity where the company's promoters are not responsible for the liability of the company. The ownership of can be transferred in the form of shares, also that taxation is under the income taxes of that company. Several other charges also impose as per the laws of the government the company must file the returns to the government. Some shares of profit must be done to the CSR. CSR is corporate social responsibility. We must allocate a small share of profit to society. Foreigners are allowed to invest in this company with the approval of that government regulations.

If you want to start a private limited company it's always better to find a business consultant to know the registration procedures, there will be some charges associated with the company's registration. So, it is always suitable for you to find a business consultant for registration and tax-related queries. The chartered accountant can create an agreement between the partners or founders of any of the firms. Today many companies are providing online company registration you can use any of the services to register your company.

11.2 Founders' agreement

This agreement is between two people in a partnership, a limited liability partnership, or a private limited company. Where both the partners or if there are more partners, they are signed towards an agreement about their positions their rules and regulation, and the allotted shares in the company so that in the future there won't be complications between the partners at any time. The founders must be given how many numbers of shares must be structured in this founder's agreement. This effective agreement will help in proper and professional functioning in the future. There won't be any objection by anyone in the company. The risk can be structured as per the company policy. If the agreement is signed by the founders, it's easy for you to start the business.

11.3 Intellectual protection

To start after you have come up with a lot of innovative ideas it is always advised to protect the intellectual protection of your company. Like patents, trademarks and there are several other things to be done while starting your business. It is like protecting your business name, the business models, and so on. You are creating a business by investing a lot of time and working on it to make a big brand. Someone objected to the future and claimed ownership of your brand. The whole struggle can be lost. There will be little complication here, but you need to protect intellectual property. Like trademarks, and patents of your products for your business ideas. The company that has these rights has a competitive advantage over others. It is easier for you to find investors. At that time if you have the proper intellectual protection, it is easy for you to get investments.

11.4 Licences

For every business and there are several licenses to be taken from the government. From any local shop to a restaurant where several environmental parameters need to be considered. A license from several boards is required to start the business. So, you must be aware of all licenses and services for you to start the business and according to the business you are into. Proper licenses must be taken before the working of the company. It is not a difficult task in taking the licenses but invests some time in knowing all the licenses required. With the help of an expert, it is so easy for you to know about the licenses and work on getting the licenses. If you are not aware of these things but if you have sacrificed a lot of time in building your business, these will be difficult for you in the future, during the bright time of your company. The licensing will change according to the different countries you are operating in and with your plan of expansion to other countries. It's always important to know the licenses of these countries. You can always seek expert advice in all these scenarios.

11.5 Labour laws

Since your company has grown to a large scale you have to know about the labor laws associated with your company. You might have a lot of employees in your company as your company expands you must provide them with PF, and gratuity as benefits. For females' maternal laws also need to be followed in your company.

At the early stage in your college start, it won't be practically possible to implement. But keep them in your mind as your team enlarges. In the long run with the help of your legal advisor or business Consultant for this labor laws must be done properly. The labor laws are created by the government to the business founder from not exploiting the people. So, it's always better to follow the labor laws as it will have benefits for your team to work with great security and help and make it a lot of confidence.

11.6 Contract management

There might be a time when you have to sign a contract like an agreement for your rental property if they are found as a partnership and so on so this contract must be effectively managed. A person must be there to look after all these at the renewal time and you must create an agreement on the right with your supplies. If you are dealing with or in any of your dealers you are dealing with this will help you in the long run to win any of the legal objections put forward by your competitors in the long run of your business. Long-term contracts with other companies can also help both companies to grow with your deals.

"Something worth doing might take a while, so really flesh out the potential of the business and be honest about whether it's worth doing. If it's not a $100 million company in five years, maybe it'll take 10 or 15 years. If you're doing something that has a universal, timeless need, then you need to think of the company in a timeless way."

Scott Heiferman

Founder / Meetup

12

INFORMATION TECHNOLOGY

Around 250 years ago industrial revolution was one of the major changes that caused or turned upside the lives of the human being. After the industrial revolution, there was something happened that again made the life of human beings easier, and it made a lot of work opportunities. This was the evolution of information, now called information technology. With information technology, we use and analyze the data using computing devices and predict some of the output and the future forecast for many businesses. When we use this information technology in the business this helps in a lot of ways to make a business easier in a scalable manner.

Since almost all human beings are present on the internet, we can showcase something to them at a low cost. That too with the help of the internet. With the help of this internet information, technology drives innovation and innovation is the path to business success. With a lot of people using this information, it is easy to put our products and to reach the targeted audience at the easiest. Business innovation had an impact on many of these Industries some of them was, that online shopping was more efficient with the help of this innovation, digital marketing is more efficient than newspaper television and other conventional marketing methods, social networking is easier than going to any of the parties or meetings to meet them, so similar things are happening around. Things like these make life easier. Cloud Computing is more efficient than a private computer network. With the help of this data, we can make different strategies through the internet.

The internet makes us easier to create business planning and to have more efficient marketing, several business opportunities arise within information technology, and also it provides support to others in the business.

12.1 Website

A website is something that can be shown as the face of a business. In the world of the internet, everyone has their presence on the internet and you being an entrepreneur must show your presence and your business presence there. If you want to search for anything go on the internet, so a website is something that displays the information in front of your customer on that internet. So, you must make a website showing your products and services even if it is not a digital product. It is always going to benefit your businesses in such a way that, if someone wants to buy similar products our website will be also there showing the product. So, if we drive a lot of traffic through this website. If we don't have any website and what if someone wants to find a product of our company how they can get into contact with the company across the world. So can anyone find the product from outside? With the help of a website so anyone can see our businesses on the internet. There are a lot of companies that make websites for other businesses also website creation is a freelancing opportunity for a lot of individuals. You can reach many of them through any of the means even through the internet and can create a website for your business and create a face for your business in the world of the internet.

12.2 Solve Complex problem

With the running of a business, there may be a lot of data generated every day and every week, and every month. We need to look at them after some period or a necessary condition. We need to make decisions based on that. A lot of complex decision-making and strategy creation can be done. If there was no building information technology and no computing devices used in business and treating them like the conventional business model it is very difficult to arrange all these data and create a great output from the information. So, this helps in great complex problem solving, you can automate a lot of your regular tasks like sending the salary with software for employees, storing their information and details, and all be done with the help of this information technology.

12.3 Better decision

With the help of Information Technology, there is a lot of data available that was not only found by yourself but also by everyone on the internet. We can find them reorder or sort them and we can use them as per our requirements. So, this helps a lot in making decision making. In any firm where many people are involved, there are a lot of risks associated with decision-making. Risks come from the lack of Information and our wrong decisions, at that time with the experience we can make better decisions at the right time. There is also a disadvantage in that In case our information is not good a lot of misinformation can lead to confusion. This confusion can stop us from doing anything also but being rational and taking decisions with the right data. We can bring in the growth of our business and the successful running of that company.

12.4 Marketing result

Before modern marketing was introduced to the world there was only conventional. During that time people use to broadcast their posters through the newspaper or television where most people see them. Today most people are spending more than half of their time on the internet with their work and their personal life so a lot of people are available on the internet, that's where the technique called digital marketing comes into the picture. Digital marketing is itself a billion-dollar Industry. Marketing using this digital means create helps businesses to create more leads at least more sales than the conventional marketing method. More people are living on the internet so creating anything inside them will create traffic to your business and helps in the growth of your company. With the help of Information Technology and digital marketing, a lot of marketing success can be created for many companies. There are many freelancers in the digital marketing sector as well as many companies providing these digital marketing services. There is something called digital marketing agencies that also provide these services. They will continuously help you to get more leads through the internet so you can use something in your marketing methods.

12.5 Resource Management

If we are relying on information technology a lot of resources can be managed through Cloud Computing. The company's employees to use any device anywhere in the world. So that if anyone wants to access any data immediately at any time, they can easily place the information in the cloud storage. This helps a lot with resource management. The use of this can have some disadvantages, the technology relies on security Part.

A lot of money needs to be invested in that. The cloud-providing companies provide their security at the highest level for their audiences to stay back. A lot of information can also be stored within the cloud that helps other people to catch their get these data a lot of information can be shared within the group of the company and within their employees with the help of the cloud management system.

12.6 Improved customer support

During the Olden times, customer support was only through the telephone there was the mail that was sent directly from the user and the companies must reply to them. This was a long day's procedure. With the help of Information Technology now there were a lot of methods so that they can get customer support if any customer-facing any problem with their products the customer care team can solve it within minutes if they can access the internet or even a direct phone call to the company and the customer executive will attend the customer. This can bring a sense of satisfaction for that customer, this helps to generate more and more traffic to your company because their trust in you has increased. Most of your products can be sold and your company can become a great success

How are you doing these things in your company is replicated in the growth of your company. Those who are using adaptive technology first will always get a higher stand in the industry. The competition of your business will get reduced as most of the work is automated. Since almost all industries are facing competition, it is important to rely more and more on technology. This provides more results with the least investment. In college, you can find a lot of learning and skilled people for doing these tasks. Without looking back, you must investigate these mentioned topics and domains as per your business requirements when you are starting your first start-up

"The desire to get press when a site/product goes live is flawed. 'News' is relative to when it is announced, not when it happened. Wait for it..." "To focus more on something you must focus less on something." "Time sorts most things out."

Scott Belsky

Co-Founder / BeHance

13

MARKETNG

Marketing is like the heart of your business because it helps your company to survive, and find the customer needs to reach the target audience this is fully in the hands of this marketing process. Several ways of marketing are done traditionally and their new ways of marketing that are done. Modern methods help you to spread the name of your company for example apple is a company for everyone to choose to buy a smartphone the first name that comes to mind is whether an Apple product or not a fruit apple this is the advantage and power of great marketing. Marketing is not a conventional set of rules which means the marketing can be done in a specific manner only. There are a lot of different ways how you can bring your product to the hand and the mind of your potential customers.

The main idea of marketing is to make others know what you are doing and show others the product you build. For that first you need is a great marketing plan. With a great plan, you can gain as many leads as possible, and retaining customers can also help you to grow your company's reputation. It says with a lot of text and images combined properly by a specialist is better than investing in another hundred people for making publicity. This comes under the creative part. The idea of marketing can alone bring a lot of changes to your company and your product. Marketing can help us to have a great face in Infront of customers with your marketing strategy and great product your customer will accept your services and products in the long run. While your marketing campaign is running always try to make up the promises given. Always try to improve customer retention and satisfaction so that you can create a steady audience and customers. Also, great marketing is through word of mouth. That is the customer saying others about their good experiences. No strategy can beat them.

13.1 Be "SMART"

Smart is the marketing term that is used to explore the specific, measurable, attainable, relevant, and timely behavior of the market which means how much specific you are in identifying your customers and the potential market. Measurable means how you can measure the impact of your marketing plan on the audience and the customer. You are approaching attaining your marketing plan, is this attainable in the near on long future? How much it is relevant? And how much output it can provide? Is your marketing plan relevant to the customer or for whom you are targeting? If your customer base is something different from what you are trying to communicate then it may be difficult to convey your message. Fair timing is an important concept in marketing, how to time the market to reach the correct audience at the right time is all-important, with the right approach you must time and plan what you are going to do in a marketing campaign. If it's not the right time, then it's better to postpone the marketing plan and must only provide the correct marketing plan at the right time.

13.2 Clear and compelling message

Before you start your marketing time you must be very clear with what you are going to show and to whom you are going to show it. If you have identified the person whom you are targeting is very easy that is the main part of marketing is done. Because now you must identify the behavior, and culture pattern of that targeted audience and you must identify the strength and weaknesses and how the purchasing power of the customer. If you can find something like that now, it's time for you to build a strategy for your business. Something strong company message and strength needs to be marketed. And your competitors must watch what you are doing. At first, when you have no experience before your job is to find their marketing plan. How they marketed and how they are targeting their audience and now it's not time for you to replicate the same and try to work something better than that. Try to gain more customers from them. If you can create a compelling message and a clear-cut marketing plan the customer with your competitors will come to you to purchase your product. The product may have competition in marketing from companies that have been established for hundreds of years. A new company coming with a new marketing plan and with a new innovative product can catch the market. The established company all started small.

13.3 Use a combination of ideas and tactics

Once we have identified the potential customers who are going to buy our products right now it's time for us to create the ideas, which may be to create an email that will convert this into a potential customer. Create a tactic which means we must create a strong strategy on how we are going to approach the people. Sometimes we must bring a model or a brand ambassador which may be known by others to a great extent. Well-known people and the words said by them will create a sense of confidence in them to buy the product they are telling. Even the color, template, and words we are using for a marketing plan are going to impact the business. The color combination is something that is creating a subconscious impact on human beings we must identify the behavior of humans.

If you are in the children's sector must not forget whom to target in this case, you must target the parent and we must create a marketing plan according to their parents, not for the children. The right marketing lives in words that connect to emotions. We make a combination of these ideas and tactics and these tactics executed properly can create more and more growth for your business at first like anything your marketing campaign can also fail, this is the worst case. But keep up the real spirit of an entrepreneur that is not giving up, work on to find where is wrong and work till you find the most suitable one now on trying to keep on improving the marketing plan till the goal is reached.

13.4 Distinguish target buyers

Once you have started the business or if it may be your first business and don't think that the whole world is your market. One of the biggest companies Amazon is contributing only to a small percentage of the total population. Being a beginner, you must target precisely whom you are serving. There may be classes among the targeted customers. You must be watching each type of user separately and with maximum concentration. So, you are not going to the wrong customer. They may be a class a customer with me buying a premium product from your site and you must create a marketing plan targeting them. This must not be used for someone who is class B and does not have the potential to buy your premium products. If you are doing this, then the marketing lead is going in the wrong direction. Understand how the people are buying and how much they are willing to spend and if the people are willing to spend more you must create a premium marketing plan to capture them, make them feel privileged, and make them comfortable in buying your product.

13.5 Social media

Back during conventional marketing when there was no internet infrastructure available was mostly used, that was mostly viable so many people prefer that conventional television marketing channels, and most of the marketing of big brands were done through television. They were able to generate a lot of popularity and publicity for their product, after 2007 or so, during this time the internet was becoming popular. Then the bandwidth is more, so more people are working, and most people are spending most of their time on social media. You must put your marketing in places where most people gathered whether it's social media or places having television channels there's nothing like that. If you are targeting an audience that is residing in social media which most probably is because almost all people have at least one social media. You must target them at least for the publicity and the popularity of your brand social media is an important source for the marketing approach must make use of social media. To create more impressions and reach you must give people what they wanted which might be like a giveaway so that you can generate leads for and get more reach for your products and services. If you are receiving fewer leads at that time also you can use this tactic to boost sales.

13.6 Distribute content

Once you have identified the potential for social media now it's time for you to distribute your content across all social media platforms where your customer finds it. The wrong thing that the marketing team does is just push it randomly. You must be very much targeted and precise while distributing content. Something that is walking on one social media channel may not work for the other. Figure out the algorithm behind that social media so that you can create something according to that by optimizing the content.

For youtube, you can create content explaining your full details regarding the product. People there will watch it because the algorithm is structured in such a way. You can use the community tab for announcements and countdowns. Similarly, Instagram also has such policies, Facebook has many features. Also, find the demographics and ages of people using the platforms.

13.7 Paid Add

Till now we have discussed the organic method of driving traffic to your products and services. We have some other methods to get a notice from other people. That is, we will be paying, and they will put our content in their feed. Such a campaign can be done either with the help of a digital marketing consultant or any social media agency, even freelancers are doing the same thing at a reasonable price. The modern times digital marketing is far cheaper than conventional marketing for a television channel at the cost of advertising is very high compared to social media. In social media, you can even run away for a few thousand rupees and even a greater level of automation is possible. You can directly capture leads and convert them into sales. With direct selling and reseller programs and you can generate leads through paid marketing and a large amount can be received through this field. Marketing can be realistic, back-to-back marketing channels can generate more and more leads. With this, your business can be automated and takes your products more viral and very soon you will get recognition for it.

13.8 Offer free trial

Once you are starting a new venture or launching a new product it is very helpful to get momentum if you can offer a free trial for people. It is always said that you put your hands on your product and if they are satisfied with our products and help them to solve any problem or make themselves better that they will want to buy. If that's not done getting access to your product by your customer is low and they won't believe that this will solve their problems. Even if you have done any other methods, self-satisfaction is always important for buying a product from the customer's perspective. This will bring in a growth in the number of sales for your company that too at the initial stage. The idea of offering a free trial is adopted by many product-based start-ups. You can also get initial feedback through this. Even if you don't get the expected initial feedback don't get dis-hearted as great products take some time to evolve.

"You need space to try things and create. It takes a long time to recalibrate if you let people pull at you all the time. A lot of stress comes from reacting to stuff. You have to keep a certain guard [up], if you're a creative person."

Pete Cashmore

Founder / Mashable

14

MARKET SIZE

One of the most crucial task entrepreneurs has witnessed is to calculate the size of the market and the potential value the market has. For start-up businesses exactly, you must determine the overall market size of your business. If you have a clear-cut idea of the market capacity. We have already discussed business competition; you might have known some competitors in this Industry. If we can identify their share in the market the amount of money, they might be getting over a period can be calculated. This data is crucial for other purposes, also when you are going for a venture capitalist for fundraising. Fundraising will be discussed in the later part of the book. If you are going in a growing market or a shrinking market everything can be determined with this data. This will influence your business. If there is no market for a product the potential funding, you might be received will be very low sometimes it will be difficult to find one.

Once you have started a business and then entering in the market now it's time for you to capture the maximum market share of your Industry try to get maximum market share at the early stage. If you can create more growth in a short period then your growth is more, this can be used as a very important factor to invite raising funds for your expansion plans. You must be very much perfect on how you are going to penetrate this market. You must be clear on how you are going to capture more and more customers and make them use your products and services. The initial plan for stepping into your business and when pitching to investors is very crucial. For fundraising this is an important factor, this will be missed if you cannot answer the question. For making the initial momentum and success by avoiding difficulty. You must understand the market share concept. The business will also get affected if you don't know the right market size of the start-up.

14.1 How to determine market size

To calculate your market size, you will be looking into the number of customers you are having and the number of transactions each year. With the total transactions and the customers available for the market, you can get the outline. You will not get the exact amount, in most cases, you will get a vague idea of the number of people, who will be using the product. If you can find at least a minimum of data, you can create a plan to hunt the market.

14.2 Total addressable market

Realistically not all start-ups should expect 100% market share unless they are operating in the rarest market. Even though it is very difficult for you to obtain a market if you can get a hundred percent market share which will be called a monopoly in that industry. Monopoly is always beneficial for the business, but it is not always beneficial from the customer's point of view. So is very unrealistic and very hard to become a Monopoly in some industries. If you can find a niche industry that can create great products and can hold the maximum market share. Still, there might be competition new people will come into seeing your traction. They can even capture the market ahead of you and this has already happened in the past. You must be determining the total addressable market in which how much you can capture from the total market. You must start and expand it by capturing more and more customers. So, you must be aware of what will be the total addressable market and enter there with your marketing and other Strategies. You can verify your growth in your business and can enlarge your business to a great extent.

"Be true to yourself. If you follow that principle, a lot of decisions are actually pretty easy."

Tony Hsieh

Founder / Zappos

15

FUNDING

While starting a business most people were getting nervous is on how they get the money required to start and run the business. Business is a form of money-making system in which people must give up on money to make ten times (more or less) the money back. In business, funding is very much important, and in the case of the start of business, the focus will be on the growth factor. A lot of funding is required for sales and marketing. Other Areas where funding is required are mainly for the expansion phase to make up the team and so on. Without funding the start-up might also feel difficulty and eventually die. Funding is almost an important part of the business, especially during the functioning of the business. In case the business cannot find or get them at the right time the effect on the business will be bad. In such cases, the employees as well as the founder of them may not be able to meet up the requirements of their customers. This creates a negative impact on the customers. The founders must have detailed financial planning as we have discussed in the above chapters before starting and approaching the business.

Make a clear idea while approaching investors, must go to them with how much money is estimated at which time of business. If there is a proper calculation of the balance sheet and cash flow of the business is very much easy to get a picture of the entire business. We can present the big picture within the business. Everything will run under a system when we have the vision to work on. Never put all your money or don't take the money which is kept for some other purposes or any other need. This led to an imbalance in the financial system of the business. If any factor of the business gets disturbed, it can affect the entire earnings of the business so in that case the finances have been very carefully handled and calculated. How to spend your money and approach investors will be discussed in the later part of this book.

15.1 Why funding is required

Funding is required for a variety of purposes here we will be discussing some of them in detail and will discuss how we can arrange the funding in the later part of this book.

The starting will be for the prototype creation for every product we have to create must first need to create an MVP also called the minimum viable product or a prototype that must be created. The prototype must be very much similar and close to the original product we are going to develop. The MVP will be different from the original product, but it must be minimum viable. It is not expensive as the prototype is not needed to create in huge quantities. We can create with minimum and least resources. The disadvantage is that if a simple prototype cannot meet the requirements, we need to create more and more prototypes. This will lead to in that more amount of money. First, we must create a great prototype with the least resources and maximum creativity then only a greater product will be born. This will be the base version of the production. For a real product, we need to incorporate features that our clients or customers wanted, everything like this can be done in production, We will make the prototype as much crystal clear that is like the product.

Once a fixed amount of money is set for prototype creation. We can now move to develop the products. With the help of the product, we can raise money from investors. For product development, we must develop the product and it must be full-fledged for which the product must be reliable and as per the business vertical. You are into product development it must fulfill all the qualities and needs and process the things that are required for the customer and product development. Set up inventory management for the product. For product development, we need some time, more land, labor, and even machinery all these come under the product development sector. A lot of money as per requirement can be kept aside for product development if we cannot develop products, we cannot sell anything.

Team hiring, the main pillar behind a Start-up is a strong team working together to achieve a common goal. So, the team needs to pick the right person at the right time for the right job to work. People must be highly skilled to complete their given work. To sustain a strong team, they must be getting paid well. We must give some money and a portion of the funding to the team. There is no point in compromising with the team hiring. If we are paying less for the team the output of the team will also be low. There is no use in giving five thousand rupees for a job that can be a fifty thousand payable job. The output of that work will decrease.

Once the business start running, we need to find the working capital and meet the day-to-day expenses and the monthly expenses. Which may be the cost of the internet, the rent, and everything. Working capital must be calculated also the increment in working capital must also be calculated and forecasted before running the business. By this, we will get clarity on the working capital and keep them aside. If the working capital gets affected by any means or by other problems or due to the lack of funding the working of the business will be affected. For other uses we must keep separate money for working capital, working capital is inevitable in the running of the business

Legal and Consulting Services are required for the company to run there may be a lot of licenses required as per the vertical of your business. In this, there may be some sectors where a lot of detailed complications to be resolved. Some of them are an airline, chemicals, and fertilizers a lot of consultation services are required and certainly need to be made throughout the running of the country. At the early stage having in-house legal and corporate advisors are difficult, outsourcing them can also account for a huge sum of money.

Once we have started with the businesses with a physical product we need raw materials, equipment, and machinery to manufacture so the manufacturing has certain expenses. To tackle this by some amount the raw materials can be purchased from the seller who is giving at a minimum price. Compare with others in giving the same raw material. In the case of equipment or machinery, we cannot compromise the quality if the quality is compromised, it will affect the end products. Raw materials and equipment will be considered the most important factor for the production and if any of them don't work there is no use with other sectors. Look into the business each point is important may be a section will be weak we need to find and fix it. So, we had to investigate deeply so that we can create a great business

Licenses and certifications, for the license application there will be several charges will is generated by the government. These charges are inevitable for a business. Once we are starting there will be a lot of money given for the licenses and certification. There will be some reasonable fees for the same somewhere may be online will be cheap than offline. This, require a lot of research and asking experienced people. In some cases, a small fraction of the money will be given for the certification, and this is meet the legal requirements. This is only valid for a limited period then we can need the renewal charges for them

Marketing, as we had a dedicated chapter for marketing it accounts for a lot of money in many businesses, and we must spend very much further for marketing. The Sales sector with this is something that takes a huge amount of money in reaching a large audience and the potential market. For marketing, a definite proportion of money must be kept aside so that it can be put on a lot of money back into the company's account.

Office space and other expenses, office spaces are required for any expenses business even a complete online business there will be expenses. Office space must be there to run a business, there is a recurring amount needed for the functioning it will also increase in some time or year. Find the best office space and the place must be accessible by many people if a lot of people are accessing the same space, then the chance of the rent is also going to increase. It's better to choose the best office space and allocate a suitable amount of funding for that space of that the customer can get direct access and won't get affected by your office and your premises

15.2 Types of funding

There are three types of start-up funding which is equity financing, debt financing, and grant.

In brief equity financing in was selling a portion of your company's equity in return for capital. The person who is holding the equity will become a part owner of that company as per the position of the equity. The owner will get the involvement and have more access to the company. There will be no component of refinement of the invested amount the money you have invested must not need to be repaired and there is also no guarantee that the investment will give the required returns in the long run. At any point in time even if the company faces loss and shuts down its service. The share value of the company will go to zero. The main advantage of this is the high capital growth for investors. Most start-ups have grown tremendously over a period and they have a lot of track records for the growth of the business. So, capital growth is something that impresses a lot of investors. Even though a lot of risks are associated with still investors prefer investing in start-ups. The reason was that among the 10 companies they were into if any one of them can become the next Google, Facebook, or tesla. The investors have a great network of smart intelligent people. With their experience and knowledge, they can pick the best start-ups.

The next type of funding is debt financing debt financing involved the borrowing of money and paying it back with the interest. You are highly reliable, and you must pay the amount back which was created at the time of the agreement. The lender has no control over the business operations. The business must pay the amount as interest to the person who is lending the money. The greatest advantage of this is that you can take money without the involvement of others in becoming the owners of the company. The disadvantage is that you have to pay the interest to the person who is lending the money in all scenarios. From an investor's point of view, the risk is compared to low as you have ensured the money is getting back. But the return will be fixed, and growth or return on investment will also be low.

The Third way of fundraising is called a grant is usually an award. The amount of money is given to a company for various reasons and at different stages to facilitate the proper starting in most cases. Some grants are for the ideation they may be given for the prototyping. There is no repayment of the invested amount, and no one will become the owner of the company. The amount of money you are getting is to make your business come to the market. Usually, grants are provided by government organizations, which help that country of the nation to get more employment and create more business opportunities in that nation. Sometimes colleges also provide such grants to budding entrepreneurs from their institutions.

"Don't be afraid to fail. My dad encouraged us to fail. Growing up, he would ask us what we failed at that week. If we didn't have something, he would be disappointed. It changed my mind-set at an early age that failure is not the outcome, failure is not trying."

Sara Blakely

Founder / Spanx

16

STEPS IN FUND RAISING

We have seen how we must calculate the funding required for running a business and what are areas where most of the funding is required from business to business and the type of business model you're following. The fund requirement sometimes requires a low amount, which may be required for operation and working. But for the expansion, the funding is required more for your company to survive and struggle so as per the business model. There are several ways to start-up up a fundraising event. There are other ways and methods for start-up fundraising, but this is the standard most of them follow and these are the criteria that are standardly accepted for us to create any fundraising program.

16.1 Assessing the need for funding

We must have a clear financial picture of the Business, and this must be for listing in charts. If possible, we must create in the next five to ten years or at least eight years at least financial plan before meeting any investor for funding. This will create a sense of confidence in you and your company in making money and other people who are ready to invest in your company. Investors are looking for your ability to make money for them and make the business put forward by you. A financial forecast must be carefully constructed, and this will help in the growth of your company's overall development. For a specific period, the market you are into the customer satisfaction you are giving, the product development process, manufacturing, everything must be well planned and how much money we must be allocated for each sector must be carefully created

16.2 Assessing investment readiness

As we have identified the requirement for finding investors you must be careful doing the thing that is required at this point. This will take the thing out and involves their hard-earned money. You must convince for revenue projection. Investors will generally investigate several factors with which they will only invest in something that can create a great return in a small period. If there are other data with you, in the investor's meeting this is going to help the investor to be convinced.

They will get the funding some of them will be looking into the revenue growth, and market position and you are showing the favourable ones. When the investors are investing at the time of break even or not even profitable. For different businesses, the time to break even will be and the time for that to become profitable will be much larger. For some companies the break-even is low and will be profitable from the beginning onwards, the uniqueness of start-up and competitive advantage is a great strategy while approaching investors. Your vision and your future are looked at by the investors and the people who are ready to invest in your start-up. If you can somehow show all these things to the person whosoever is interested in investing in your start-up, then you are more likely to get the funding.

16.3 Preparation of business

A picture of a detailed presentation, about the starting and outlining all the important aspects of your start-up is the first thing to prepare. Creating an investor pitch is all about telling a good story. You tell your story and convince them that you can make your opinion into reality, that is when you will find success in getting funding. You may not get it right in the first pitch you need to work till you get the right one. We can attain the output of your pitch experience. You can create a great business for investors, and you can have a huge amount of money.

16.4 Investor Targeting

While you are seeking investment from a venture capitalist or any individual fund-raising company. You are not only getting money but also their expertise in your business. You must identify which investors can help you and how they can help you in achieving something for growth. The network of the venture capitalist will be very high compared to how much other businessmen have. You might have a small network, so it's an important resource for which investor is putting money into your company. While you are looking for investors it will be difficult for you to pitch the idea to other investors because they may not be aware of the geographic location and the culture of your customer. You must be careful while selecting a venture capitalist as your efforts may get wasted initially. There may be a lot of confusion in the fundraising process but with time you will get more and improved results in the future.

16.5 Venture capitalists and Angel investors

Venture capitalists and Angel investors will look at the start-up's past financial decisions, the team's credentials as well as the background of the founders. They look for the product market fit with your experience in creating a Start-up. For a college start-up, it might be difficult for you to show your personal experience and claim that you can capture the market and the numbers can be achieved within your period. You must create another strategy that might work for you. Someone from your network can sometimes help with this. Your pitching will be possible with time.

16.6 Term sheet

The term sheet is a non-binding test of opposition by a venture capital firm. At the earliest date, you will be summarising the major points of engagement on how you are linked with the investor and the start-up. The term sheet for the venture capitalist typically consists of four structural provisions depending on the country they may change. The most common structure provisions evaluation on valuation structure, management structure, investment structure, and finally changes to share capital.

16.6.1 Valuation

Valuation is the total worth of a company. This is met by professional values valuation depending on how much money the company is creating and how much time with which it is achieved. With their relevant time and with the inventory and assets owned by the company. Business valuation is something for each share a shareholder is owning how much the company can create and in general, will create the share value of that company. The all-share value of all the shares in the company will get that company valuation. There are several methods to value a company such as the discounted cash flow method for a market multiple processes and so on valuation can always increase as the business grows and the investors see that the difference has the potential to grow even further that's why many investors and investing in start-ups for their growth.

16.6.2 Investment structure

Investment structure defines the mode of venture capital investment, whether it is through equity or the combination of debt as we have mentioned earlier. The advantages and disadvantages of equity and debt and how you are going to raise the money are considered as the investment structure

16.6.3 Management structure

The management structure of the company includes the list of the board of directors. The prescribed appointment and removal procedures and how the company is structured and who are under each category. So, the rules and regulations are described under this part of the term sheet

16.6.4 Changes to share capital

All investors in start-ups have their investment timelines and accordingly they seek flexibility while investing they seek exit options from their investments, and most investors have a priority in the exit option. Some of them receive some years ahead so they want a great extent of profits and now they can transfer the shareholder's right and obligation to the new shareholders all comes under this part of the term sheet.

"Learn public speaking. Of all the skills that an entrepreneur can have, I think the ability to convey an idea or opportunity, with confidence, eloquence and passion is the most universally useful skill. Whether you're pitching a group of investors, rallying your employees, selling a customer, recruiting talent, addressing customers, or doing a press tour, the ability to deliver a great talk is absolutely invaluable. And it is perhaps THE most under-recognized and under-nurtured skill."

Tim Westergren

Founder / Pandora

17

INVESTORS POINT OF VIEW

Investors are people who have a lot of money with them, and they are willing to invest their money into young businesses called start. The advantage they are getting is the start of such exponential growth over their money. They are expecting a great return on their investment within a few years. The disadvantage they are facing is that only one or two start-ups among a hundred will be successful in their portfolio but in general if one company gets successful, they can multiply the money by 'n' times, they are taking that much risk for getting that return. When investors are looking for a start-up, they look for various elements, and if you can make up with these things you can find a great investment in your company. A great investment is not only with the money but also by the support and network of the investors and their working power expand your product and company because it was also now of their company by buying a stake in your company.

17.1 Objective and problem solving

The start-up must provide a differentiated and unique way to solve any customer problem. It must meet any specific consumer needs with ideas or products that are patented or have any moat that shows high growth potential for investors. The position of the company while you are pitching to the investors will create a sense of confidence in you in dealing with your products and with the problems faced by your customers.

17.2 Management and team

The experience, passion, and scale of the team working in the management will drive the company toward success. Investors look great into the strength of the management and the team. During the start of the investing period if you can find a great team working together to achieve a common goal and solve a problem in the real world it will be a great advantage for you to pitch to your investor and get a suitable return.

17.3 Market landscapes

This means the market you are trying to get into has growth potential. The market growth and the historical record of the market will be taken into consideration. They will also sometimes investigate the competition and the market leader who are already established in the market. If your company has a strong barrier to entry into a particular market, it becomes a red flag in getting investment for your company. This market landscape is enough by area for you to get the investment. There is a solution for its strategy to tackle the market and if you can prove that your strategy is to work with proper guidance and support, this will be helpful in you to make your desired outcome.

7.4 Customers and suppliers

The investor will be looking for a customer as well as a supplier who will be providing the raw materials as per the business you are into. For some businesses, customers are the most important. If you find that the customers are weak, they can migrate to some other competitors. If you have any long-term relationship with the suppliers or distributor and it is always an added benefit for your company and the supplier's loyalty can also be pitched to your investors

7.5 Scalability and sustainability

Credibility and sustainability are two main important factors that can give validation to your business over a long period. If your products are scalable to all regions of the world and it is sustainable so that they can last for a long period then it has an advantage for your company. Scalability can be done in many ways and if the stability factor is dependent on some of the most inclusive methods, then it will be difficult. You must find the potential for your idea and how much it must be scalable and sustainable in the long run. If any of the major economic black swan events are happening in the world. It must not affect strongly to your business, and this will cost for sure some advantage for your business.

17.6 Competitive analysis

I have mentioned earlier for every business you are starting they might be competition. It is difficult to find a market where there is no competition. If there a low competition in the market it means that the market might be diminishing and by that sustaining, in the long run, is difficult. So competitive analysis comprises all the competitors in a particular market and analysing the strengths and weaknesses and finding the opportunity among all of them. If you can find any added competitive advantage for your business or your product for your customer. Then it's always a benefit for you to speak in front of the investors and convince them.

17.7 Sales and marketing

Sales and marketing at the two methods by which the overall effort of the business comes to an end which will bring money to your company. Rest all the activities will take money from your company to outside. So, these are the two main pillars of the businesses from the investor's point of view, they will investigate the numbers for sales and the strategies you are using for marketing. You Must also have a competitive advantage compared with your competitors. If you can show it's a great number in sales their sales growth percentage and the profit margin it's easy for investors to invest in your business. Because you are running a money-making business and investors are always attracted to places where money is made. They will invest strongly in your company if you can create a great sale with fewer liabilities for your company.

17.8 Exit Avenue

When investors are trying to get into the business, they always look for the exit avenues of the exit path. They wanted to make the maximum return on the money they have invested in a short period. There are various methods for exiting a start-up like the initial public offering, where the company will be going public the public will be buying and selling the share of the company. By this method, the early investors will be getting a huge premium for the money they paid at the beginning.

If our business is acquired by some other companies or we get an alliance partner, this becomes a valuable decision for exit strategies. If your company has great potential in any of these things the investors will be impressed with your company.

In this chapter we have discussed the various method in which how investors are looking to invest for a start-up this is applicable for start-ups and as per the business model you are creating. In the market you are in you must provide these in your favor. You must always showcase your advantages over your disadvantages don't hesitate to show your disadvantages to the investors because from their experience you might get some support in overcoming and solving your problems.

"It's hard. And just when you think it can't get any worse, it does. There'll be times when it just keeps getting worse and worse and worse. Meanwhile, everyone else around you is getting better and happier and richer. You'll feel like the only one who hasn't figured it out yet. You're sinking, your life sucks, and your business isn't going anywhere. Oh yeah, and you're not getting any younger, either. And just when you think about finally throwing in the towel, and saying "first all this!" that right there is the test that all founders are eventually faced with: when things get too hard, you decide to stay, or you decide to quit. My advice is this: Before you decide, look at all those great, successful businesses that inspired you to start your own. They stayed."

Ben Chestnut

Founder / Mail Chimp

18

FAILURE AREAS

Starting a business is a lot harder than most people think we need to incorporate a lot of things to run a business. We have learned so far to run a successful business and if we have done all these properly it is still possible for the business to fail miserably. Once you have started a business it is very much important to calculate the risk associated with the business. If you are putting all your hard-earned money and if the business doesn't go out if all your product does not get sold out and you must be ready to accept the failure and prepare for your next move. In this chapter, we will be discussing the main reasons for the failure of start-ups that have occurred in the past. For us when we are starting a business this will most probably come before us. The thing that we are doing might be wrong. Sometimes it takes a lot of time to determine it.

The most common mistake is we are not ready to accept failure at the early point at the time of ideation or so. We think that our idea is the most and we will be the best in the market. Understand the fact that everyone in your industry is running behind a similar goal. There is no certainty that your decisions are the right ones, for most cases, this is not possible. You need to work on making your decisions right by working on it by removing the areas of failure. The term failure might create a negative impact on everyone, especially when we are working hard to build our dreams. We must understand all the failure areas that had occurred in history. In case we can learn from others' mistakes and do not bring them into our business we have to make sure that our business will not fail in the same crisis. Some other businesses at some point in time faced this issue and later shut down.

18.1 No market need

When we have classified the reason for failure, among all other reasons, for most failures in the start-up ecosystem the main reason is that no market needs your products. You might be creating a product for a specific set audience but if your target audiences have some other better alternative than the product is providing, they will not choose your product. Ultimately many products will not get sold out in the market. Your product will fail, and this led to the trapping of your business. Usually, a start-up at an early stage has only one or two products. There might not be a wide variation of products. If they could not sell and bring back money into the company the business will fail miserably due to financial tightness. To overcome this, we just need to create something that the audiences and the customer need. Try to make products that the customer is dying to get, for example, products of Apples. While launching a new product people are running to buy give their money and buy the product. I am not asking you to make the apple, but make sure that your customer needs the product that makes an emotional attachment to your company or your products from your customers.

18.2 Run out of cash

This is faced by most businesses and starts up at the early stage. They will run out of their cash, and they could not even pay their employees. The business may not be able to get the tools and equipment needed for them. If your product is successful and if you run out of money you won't be able to meet the demand. If the company had taken a lot of debt and are wanting to repay a lot of money, then the company might run out of cash. This happens because of not proper utilization and allocation of money. That is why in the financial section we have seen in detail how to manage your finances. We must be focused and clear while managing our finances. This will not make the business run out of cash. But still, some Black Swan events can occur in business, and we must be ready to face those things.

18.3 No right team

The team is an important aspect of every start-up. We have discussed how to form a team and how to work with them. If we could not make the right time and could not find the right talent for any work, it is very difficult for running. Also, the culture of the company determines that team culture. If the culture is not proper the team will not synchronize with each other and cannot make a great output for the company. Team issue is an important reason for the failures of business. While you are creating it make sure you are hiring the right people, right people do not mean only people with the right knowledge but also having the right culture and can make up towards the mission of the company to reality.

18.4 Cost issues

They might be a lot of cost issues for your products. The raw materials provided by the suppliers may be high. If your supplier is selling at a higher price, you could not make or reduce the price and sell your final product at a lower price. You must negotiate with your suppliers and find the supplier who is providing less money. That will be beneficial for you and your products could manage the cost issues. If the price point of your product is premium and you could not deliver what your customer wanted, then the customer will be disappointed. Sometimes your competitor might be provided with a lesser amount, and you could not compete with them in the price point. This will be a black mark for the failure of a start-up.

18.5 Poor products

While starting when you are developing a product or service, if the quality is poor the customer will not use it. People always wanted value for the money they are spending. Depending on the geographical area people's attitudes towards products are also different. If you could not manage to make up for their expectations your business might fail, eventually is there are selling a product for hundred rupees you must at least provide the value of hundred and ten or hundred and twenty then only the customers will be happy business is the game of emotion between your products and your potential customer. If you can make them happy, they will be giving more money to you. Your goal in sales is to tackle the emotions of the customer while creating a product and selling. Create strong products which bring on value to the company and provide value to the customer.

18.6 Ignore customers

When the business is booming and your model of product development is ready to reach, you might be putting your hands on the marketing and other technical aspects of your business at that time you might be forgetting about the customer. This is a reason for the failures of the start-up. You are not focused on the customers and building business around it. Your business might fail eventually. You must be very much conscious of who you are as a customer and care about their changes. As we have mentioned in the earlier chapters you must get the right audience and treat customers like a king.

18.7 Product Mis-timed

This is not a big reason for start-ups, this accounts for a lower percentage among the other failure reasons. For the start-up, you will be creating a product that will be suitable for one a specific type or range of people. You might be creating a product that will be useful only in the long future and not usable now. That is called product mistimed. Being entrepreneurs, it is our responsibility to never make our business fail. You must time the market and provide customers with satisfying products. You must also make changes and gives addition to your products so that you can retain the customer for your business.

18.8 Lack passion

Passion is something that will drive every entrepreneur to work to create a business and run them smoothly every day, week, and minute. If you lack passion and your focus changes to something else, then there might be a chance of the failure of your start-up. You must work more than anybody else in your company. Where you must put on a lot of dedication and passion towards your work. You had to sometimes learn from people around you and must put in hours and hours of work daily to make keep your business alive. When your passion and commitment drain you will be felt less passionate and will reflect in the output of your business. Being an entrepreneur think about how you are going to change the life of people with your products and services. How much worth of experience you are getting from this area of business, will lead you to stay motivated and work towards the mission.

18.9 Legal challenges

When you are starting a Start-up according to the business domain may need a lot of licensing documentation and so on. But for some businesses, a lot of licensing is required and a lot of complexity in approving the businesses from the bureaucracy and the license approval at the right time this leads to a legal challenge. Not all entrepreneurs will face the same, some start-ups face these legal challenges and face fat loss exactly due to this. They will run out of cash and will eventually fail this is called the legal challenges failure reason you can create a legal team if possible, for your company to handle all the legal challenges even you can outsource these to other people or agencies.

Apart from what we have discussed above, there can be other reasons for your start-up to face difficulty. These are the main factors reasons for the failure of a start-up. You must be aware of all these things and try to not come up with such issues in your business. If you can learn from others' mistakes that half the work of success is done. If you don't you have to learn from your failures by trial and error. For such things, so you must be ready to learn from others' mistakes. What others have done wrong with their business and why they did that is all a learning opportunity.

"You have a viable business only if your product is either better or cheaper than the alternatives. If it's not one or the other, you might make some money at first, but it's not a sustainable business."

Jim Koch

Founder / Samuel Adams

19

MAKE UP WITH ACADEMICS

This chapter is not for all start-up founders but for someone who is going to start up in their college or school. A start-up might be a reason why you have chosen this book. If you have reached here pat yourself on the back. You are reading this now because you have taken immense confidence, and you have shown interest in the world of business. This is not possible for all people. Many people wish to start their businesses. And thereafter they will go to their old lifestyle and end up in their comfort zone. This does not mean business is something that is not possible but with the right guidance and knowledge, it is possible to reduce the risk of failure. We have learned a lot regarding business so far and we can implement these practical steps in our businesses. We much structure and framework out since morning incorporating all these challenges that can occur in the future.

This chapter is not about business knowledge, but it will be an insight to students in colleges to start a business during their college time. I started my first business when I was in college it was a complete online internet business and I have created the business model in such a way that the entire business can be done by myself and automating a lot of work to technology. When you are in college you must make up for that exam, test, attendants and so on. You must work extremely hard your teachers may or may not be helping in this chapter we will be telling about the strategies to work with your academic

From my experience, it is always better to start once when you are in college in your 20s because there are a lot more career opportunities ahead of you. If you are starting in academics see if you can find out whether the business is your cup of tea. Also, you can know if it's not. Then you can go to find other jobs with others. You can also take up jobs based on the degree you are receiving. It is very much helpful to trust your hard work and your effort in making a business.

Once you are in your college you must make sure that you were known by your teacher, for the amount of work you put into getting things done, if they can understand what you are doing then most probably, they will help you to achieve what you need. As we have mentioned in the early chapter, with their help with a network you will get out of many problems. Make sure that your teachers and knowledge of your start-ups and Ventures

You must individually observe people around you. That might be in your family or friends circle. You can find the right potential people, who might have at least some sort of business interest around them and want to work with you. If you feel you find the right guy, always ask them to work with you. If they are passionate and not working for money, then make sure that he is working for experience and exposure. He can become an asset to your company.

If you have understood the business and how to start a business and how to run them then it's always hard for you to share your knowledge with other students but don't hesitate to share them. Conduct seminars and webinars in your institute also help them to get into the world of the start-up. There might be a risk in business above all jobs in the world. But it is providing the highest return of all. Make others aware of the associated risks and rewards.

Try to work on your academics within a short period don't try to learn from the professors themselves you must try to learn yourself. If you have the potential to figure out a business, then you make up the academics on your own. Business needs a lot of time to be invested in running and making it into success. You won't get a lot of time attending the classes and a lot of classes will be missed. So, you must make up your own. You can use the internet because most of the academics and outdated and people are learning what is available on the internet. You find the sources and invest a lot of small portions of time and create a great score from the time you are investing.

Once the table is set, begin explaining your solution. Regardless of how intricate and complicated your solution is, explain it in simple terms to help the user understand.

The more colourful, meaningful, and simple you make the explanation, the easier time your audience will have in understanding. Keep it brief and relevant – outlining every distinct feature of your product will start to

Burn through the user's attention span and

excitement

20

CONCLUSION

College start-ups provide you with an immense opportunity that you will not receive anywhere else. Try to do it following what we have learned so far from this book. There may be hard times in front of you. It is difficult until you solve them. Become a problem solver. By solving a lot of problems that you witness this skill will become a part of your life.

From your personal life also, you can use the skills that you acquire during your business phase. You will become a talented, young, business-minded, hardworking, dedicated, passionate young man.

I would like to know about your venture. If possible, try to email me the details of your college start-up if you found this book helpful in your business journey and help in improving business knowledge.

Email id: amalrajesh01@gmail.com

Made in the USA
Columbia, SC
22 October 2022